Literacy is not enough

MANCHESTER
UNIVERSITY PRESS

Literacy is not enough

Essays on the importance of reading

Edited by Brian Cox
with an introduction by Eric Bolton

Reading is a form of friendship
Marcel Proust

Language is the soul's ozone layer and
we thin it at our peril
Sven Birkerts

Manchester University Press
and Book Trust

Manchester and New York
Distributed exclusively in the USA by St. Martins Press

Published by Manchester University Press
Oxford Road, Manchester M13 9NR, UK
and Room 400, 175 Fifth Avenue, New York, NY 10010, USA

http://www.man.ac.uk/mup

Distributed exclusively in the USA by
St. Martin's Press, Inc., 175 Fifth Avenue, New York,
NY 10010, USA

Distributed exclusively in Canada by
UBC Press, University of British Columbia, 6344 Memorial Road,
Vancouver, BC, Canada V6T 1Z2

British Library Cataloguing-in-Publication Data
A catalogue record for this book is available from the British Library

Library of Congress Cataloging-in-Publication Data applied for

ISBN 0 7190 5669 1 paperback

First published 1998

06 05 04 03 02 01 00 99 98   10 9 8 7 6 5 4 3 2 1

Printed in Great Britain by Redwood Books, Trowbridge

Contents

Foreword
Brian Cox

In 1969, I helped to edit the Black Papers on education which called for a return to structure and order in the classroom. In a television debate my opponent pointed out triumphantly that some of our contributors disagreed with each other. Naive and unaccustomed to television, I was bewildered that he should expect 20 highly educated and intelligent people to agree on all points on a subject so controversial as education policy. His attitude reflected the authoritarian simplicities of extreme progressives in the 1960s. He also knew that in television debates it is unwise to admit to uncertainties. Simple strongly-worded confidence wins the argument.

The contributors to this collection are all passionately devoted to the cause of reading. They believe literacy is not enough, that all children should develop what Richard Hoggart calls 'critical literacy'. They disagree at times on how reading should be taught and in what conditions it flourishes. Each author in this collection is responsible for his or her own opinions, and for no one else's.

In the last two decades we have witnessed a considerable reaction to the progressive Utopianism of the 1960s. All over the English-speaking world, from Australia to the United States to Canada to Britain, the talk is now about competition, league tables, the demands of the market. This reaction has gone too far. In their varying ways the contributors to this collection are demanding a revival of the traditional values of a liberal education. Children and students should be encouraged to discriminate, to evaluate, to assess evidence and to read 'critically'. Most English teachers believe that the study of English language and literature contributes to personal growth, the development of a creative imagination and an open mind resistant to propaganda. They are not going to be attracted to a profession which limits their functions to training in mechanical skills.

I welcome the Government's initiative in promoting a National Year of Reading. I welcome the determination to improve basic standards of literacy, to provide young people with the skills needed for work. I hope that the Government will recognise the urgent need to spend more money on libraries and on books in schools. I also hope that the Government will acknowledge that its policy on the teaching of reading is too prescriptive, authoritarian and mechanistic. The National Year of Reading will prove a great success if government advisers listen to experienced, professional English teachers, well represented in this collection, and send advice to teachers which is more flexible, not narrowly focused on mechanical tests. The country has large numbers of dedicated, hard-working, successful teachers of reading; the Government needs to say this again and again and again, and to listen to their views. There needs to be more emphasis on motivation, on helping children to enjoy reading. In this collection, Terry Furlong reminds us that many children master the mechanics of reading by the age of eight or nine, but then get stuck on a plateau from which they do not continue to progress. They do not read for pleasure. The problem urgently needs a less rigid curriculum, one that allows gifted teachers to adopt a variety of methods to help children to enjoy reading. Our teacher-contributors are also convinced that present methods of assessment hamper true progress in reading standards, and this issue is addressed in Bethan Marshall's essay.

Book Trust, which is sponsoring this collection, has had considerable success with its Bookstart programme. Bookstart explores the significance of the role of parents and carers in sharing books with very young children. The initial Bookstart pilot scheme concentrated on 300 parents/carers of nine-month-old babies. They were given a gift book and advice and information about books and reading by their health worker, and have been monitored (alongside a control group) over the past five years. Early results from Professor Barrie Wade and his team at the University of Birmingham indicate a substantial increase in awareness of books, sharing of books, enrolment of babies in libraries, use of book clubs and family use of books. This is the kind of research which, properly funded, can make a significant change in reading habits. All such developments must be based on research, not emotional beliefs, which too often determine attitudes to the teaching of reading.

Undoubtedly the rapid development of new media is changing reading habits, indeed human perception itself, and the essays by Valentine Cunningham, Sven Birkerts and Colin MacCabe all address this extraordinarily complex problem. I am particularly pleased by the attacks on relativism in these essays, that sickness which so harmed the teaching of English in the universities in the 1970s and 1980s. Valentine Cunningham writes: 'Literary theory has reached a pretty pass when it lacks the means to discriminate between *Bleak House* and some amusing graffito story scratched on the back of a lavatory door, or the extremely similar confessions that pack the Internet, when it fails to define the textual differences between some rock video and *War and Peace*.' Major books from Harold Bloom's polemical *The Western Canon* (1994) to Helen Vendler's superb *The Art of Shakespeare's Sonnets* (1997) are committed to the view put forward simply and forcibly in Eric Bolton's Introduction: '... some books are better than others, and that why, and how they are better, can be demonstrated.'

In the rapidly changing circumstances in which children are reared it is wrong to impose an out-of-date notion of Englishness. One contributor to this collection teaches in a school where 80 per cent of the pupils are Muslim. In the 1989 Cox National Curriculum we put forward two basic principles for the choice of books for reading in schools. First, we recommended that all pupils should be introduced to great English literature written before 1900, particularly Shakespeare. In this collection A. S. Byatt writes most powerfully about the organic growth of the English language, the urgent need for an appreciation of the insights enshrined in the literature of the past. As Colin MacCabe argues, writing for television demands high standards in the use of English: 'Those who work in the new media are anything but illiterate; the skills of reading and writing are central to all production of the new media.' The development of television does not reduce the importance of English. Ability to use English fluently and sensitively confers power, and such skills are considerably enhanced by immersion in previous literature.

We also recommended that all children should encounter and find pleasure in literary works written in English – particularly new works – from different parts of the world, from India to Nigeria to the United States. John Wilks provides a list of such authors. All pupils need to be aware of the richness of experience offered by writing in English from different countries so that they may be introduced to the ideas and feelings of countries different from their own, and so we may help the cause of racial tolerance.

Behind these recommendations lies a vision of society. We need national unity, for the development of literacy, for the common understanding of Standard English, for common values so we may live at peace with each other. We need to maintain our cultural heritage which places great emphasis on individual freedom of expression. At the same time, we need to respect local differences, the need for diversity in our multicultural society, so that we may respect each other's dialects, each other's culture, each other's religion. It is this tension between unity and diversity to which the Cox Report addressed itself. The balances it proposes are not easy to achieve, and need continual re-evaluation. We were attacked by the Right Wing, who want stability and unity based on the hegemony imposed by the upper and middle classes in the 1930s and before. We were attacked by the Left Wing because we advocated that all children should study Shakespeare and the literature of the past, our English inheritance, and that they should speak and write Standard English. I remain unrepentant. British society in the next century must develop this balance between unity and diversity. This should be the aim of all political parties. It should be central to all programmes for the teaching of reading.

Introduction: why books matter
Eric Bolton

As Chairman of Book Trust, and writer of this introduction, I suppose it is self-evident that I believe books matter, and will continue to do so for the foreseeable future. In trying to pin down why I believe that, I found my own beginnings as a reader coming to mind.

I remember when I first realised I could read, although I can't swear my exact age at the time. I know it was before I started school, but not long before. It was one of those rare 'Eureka' moments in life, but also very frustrating. Suddenly I could make sense of the lines and squiggles on the page, but no one would believe me. I don't remember my parents reading to me, though I suppose they must have done. My sister read fairy stories and poems to me, and I especially remember *La Belle Dame Sans Merci* and Old Meg. She was nearly seven years older and, to my eyes, hugely competent and confident. To ape and impress her I had been pretending for some time that I could read by going through the physical motions with stories and rhymes I knew by heart. She knew what was going on and refused to believe I could read until I had coped, more-or-less effectively, with an unseen text! From then on, hooked as I was on some of what books make possible, I became increasingly in control of what I read.

For me, given those beginnings, fiction and poetry were always dominant. Growing up in a working-class home on a council estate in which there were some, but not many, books, the branch library played a key role. The library was in the nearby secondary modern school, and, grand as it sounds, was, in fact, a set of cupboard-like book stacks in the school hall, divided into a children's and an adult section, and open three nights a week after school hours. My memories of early reading are vague, but it seems to have been a rag-bag of legends and myths, Rupert Bear, Ridley's *Believe it or Not* and, above all, comics. The weekly editions of, first *The Beano* and *The Dandy*, and later *The Adventure*, *The Wizard*, *The Rover* and *The Hotspur*, were the common cultural capital, and units of barter and exchange, of all the boys I knew. Unlike the comics of today, those for older boys consisted of page after page of columns of small print, which everyone then seemed able to read. Literary merit aside, stories about Wilson, the immortal athlete, and Click-a-Bah, the awesome cricket bat that could split a villain's skull as easily as cut a ball to the square-leg boundary, melded with Peter Pan, Ratty, Toad, Bilbo Baggins, Gandalf, Jim Hawkins, Long John Silver and Gulliver. Later on, Bulldog Drummond, Richard Hannay,

Tarzan, The Toff and Lord Peter Wimsey jostled with Oliver Twist, Pip and Estella, Tarka the Otter and Salar the Salmon.

It was not an early reading list to find favour with Queenie Leavis, or today with Young Book Trust, but it had quality dotted within it. As time passed, the formulaic repetition of many of the adventure and detective stories gave ground to the deeper and complex pleasures of more challeng-ing and satisfying books. Life and reading combined to reveal that pleasure was more complex than fun; satisfaction craved more than having one's prejudices stroked, and there was some relationship between effort made and pleasure gained.

As hobbies and interests developed and were shared with friends, reading about them in books and magazines was far and away the main route to greater understanding, knowledge and satisfaction. In my case those devel-opments were helped along by an older sister besotted by books, discover-ing herself and 'brave new worlds' as a scholarship girl at the Girls' High School; through BBC Radio's Children's Hour; a couple of perceptive teachers, and as a grammar-school boy, arguing the toss about an ever-widening collection of writers and books with friends and contemporaries.

One way or another, it was difficult to be in the swim with friends, or to inform and entertain oneself, without engaging significantly and exten-sively with books of one kind or another. Whatever we believe to be the continuing value of books, that is no longer the case. It is possible to be rea-sonably well informed about what is going on in the world, and be enter-tained, without books, or reading anything very much. The substance of the shared culture of children today is more likely to come from TV, films, video, electronic games and 'pop-culture' than from books.

When we argue the case for books and what they have to offer today, we have in mind the richness, pleasures and satisfactions of our own life-long reading experience, and the importance to individuals and society of its continuance. Like the traveller in Cavafy's poem *Ithaca* we feel 'wealthy with all we've [sic] gained along the way', and want others to enjoy the same.

But there are powerful voices that claim that books are old technology, on their way to obsolescence in the current world of the Internet, CD-ROMs and videos, let alone the promise of that which is yet to come – interactive digital TV, unlimited channels and accessible, wall-to-wall vir-tual reality. In the light of all that, those of us speaking out for books need to ask whether we are peddling nostalgia, or have a case to make about a future for books founded on what they make possible that would disappear if they ceased to exist.

I believe there is such a case to be made, but in making it we must neither tilt at windmills, nor create monsters where none exist, such as the false antithesis between new information technology and books. Again Cavafy catches the mood:

> Laistrygonians, Cyclops,
> wild Poseidon – you won't encounter them
> unless you bring them along inside your soul,
> unless your soul sets them up in front of you.
> (*Ithaca*, C. P. Cavafy)

There are more than enough real monsters without inventing them. Those include the general 'dumbing down' manifest in slipshod claims that it doesn't matter what children read as long as they read something, and the political correctness that rails against making quality distinctions between books on the grounds that such discrimination is elitist. More specific dragons to be faced include:

- literacy drives that stop short of addressing the issues of reading for meaning and the development of critical literacy, in the belief that they will come later. Yet it seems self-evident that, if by the age of seven after literacy hours and phonic drills, children have discovered no more than that the cat sat on the mat, they are unlikely to become lifelong readers;
- teachers, especially primary teachers, whose training has failed to equip them to make distinctions between the good and meretricious in selecting and using books with and for children;
- the fashionable tendency to lump all print together as information, or data, including fiction, poetry and plays, and then 'prove' the obsolescence of the book by eulogising the data-handling efficiency and effectiveness of IT;
- low spending on books by schools (less than £5 per pupil per year in a lot of primary schools); funding, resource and time problems in the library service causing closures, reductions in opening times, the demise of school library services, and the quantitative and qualitative decline in book stocks.

More positively, even in today's high-tech world, the case for books is strong. They are hugely user-friendly, fitting easily into a bag or pocket, calling for neither specialised jargon nor expensive updating, and allowing instantaneous fast forward and recapitulation. They nurture and exercise our imaginations, enabling each reader to engage personally with the text, and to pass through 'magic casements, opening on the foam /Of perilous seas, in faery lands forlorn' (*Ode to a Nightingale*, Keats).

Uniquely, books trade in and through language. Often what is happening with and to the language is as, or more, important than what is going on in plot and characters. Films made of books, however excellent as films, have a hole at their centre because what the language was up to is missing, or seriously impoverished. The film of Joyce's *Ulysses* includes some good dramatic scenes but misses out all the wonderful virtuosity of the language; even the excellent filming of Henry James' *The Wings of the Dove* is diminished by the absence of, or any filmic correlative for, James' queasily circumlocutory way with words. Pervading all that is the case for quality books and the development of critical literacy. That is especially important in the year the Government is to launch The National Year of Reading, which is intended to touch and influence the whole population. The vast majority of that population is literate, and regularly reads some kind of printed material. Consequently, while tackling illiteracy is vastly important, it can only be a relatively small part of what is to happen during the National Year of Reading, and it is reasonable to ask what is intended for the vast majority of readers. Surely that can only be to persuade them to read more; to read more widely; to read differently, and/or to read more discriminatingly. Doing any or all of that will mean accepting that some books are better than others, and that why, and how they are better, can be demonstrated.

If one of the aims of the National Year of Reading is to encourage lifelong reading it will, in part, need to enable current readers to distinguish between the worthwhile and the meretricious. Especially important is the need to help parents and teachers gain the confidence and competence to recognise quality when choosing children's books, and to do so without patronising, or alienating them. It must also aim to help many more readers understand that plot and subject matter are not all that matter. All books about boys and girls and dogs and horses are not equally good. Disney's version of *The Jungle Book*, good as it is, loses much in order to more immediately entertain, and Mills & Boon are not in the same business as the Brontës, D. H. Lawrence and John Donne. Those latter three grapple with the complexity of things, as in Auden's poem *As I walked out one evening,* where young love, 'I'll love you, dear, I'll love you / Till China and Africa meet, / And the river jumps over the mountain /And salmon sing in the street', to survive, has to withstand the inexorable passing of time, 'Time watches from the shadow /And coughs when you would kiss', and its own darker side, 'As the tears scald and start; / You shall love your crooked neighbour / With your crooked heart'.

Better writers face, and seek to come to terms with, the human condition, and help readers to do so. As Nietzsche said in *The Birth of Tragedy*, 'Art forces us to gaze into the horror of existence, yet without being turned to stone by the vision.' Arguing the importance of engaging with such unflinching integrity in what we read, and recognising its imposters, is much too important to be dismissed as 'Lit. Crit.' or cultural elitism. It seems we interpret ourselves, other people, and the world around us, through narrative. If we do read each other like books, it is likely that the narratives we read influence those we create for our own use. That being so, our narratives, those on which we build our relationships, shape our behaviour and determine action, had better be influenced for all our sakes by narratives of integrity, humanity and intelligence, rather than by the dehumanising, formulaic shock-horror and/or sentimentality of much pulp fiction. There are good and bad books, and it cannot be gainsaid that some of what books do can now be done better by other media. In the end what remains unique is the medium itself – the printed word – and the complex inter-relationship between form and substance. All we readers have are words on a page, and the baggage we bring with us. We are forced to use our imaginations to envisage the characters and the worlds evoked by the writers, and must attempt to get into the hearts and minds, and under the skins, of the protagonists. That ability to empathise with others, to put ourselves in their place, is, it seems, emerging from recent studies of primates, as probably the single characteristic that distinguishes humankind from the beasts. If that is so, the more sensibly and sensitively we are able to do it, the more truly human we become. As Wordsworth claimed in *The Prelude*, it is 'Imagination, which in truth / Is but another name for absolute power / And clearest insight, amplitude of mind, / And Reason in her most exalted mood' that makes that possible. Of course, it is not only books that stimulate and educate our imagination, but they do it in particular ways, and in a particularly accessible form, that could not be replicated should they be lost to us.

To adapt Bill Shankley, the legendary manager of Liverpool Football Club, who once said that football was not a matter of life and death: it was much more important than that; books are not about literacy, or data storage and retrieval. They are much more important than that; they are about life and death. Good, and great books, seriously and memorably so. The meretricious offer up sensation for its own sake, stereotypical characters and tired formulaic plots. Consequently, if, as an open society, we are to value, succour and enhance what books uniquely make possible, and show by our actions that books matter, we *must* accept that all books are not equally defensible, and engage with questions of quality and discrimination.

Part 1   *Reading matters*

Aesthetic criticism returns us to the autonomy of imaginative
literature and the sovereignty of the solitary soul, the reader not as
a person in society but as the deep self, our ultimate inwardness.
Harold Bloom

The exaltation that comes from certain kinds of reading has a
propitious influence on our own work; more than one writer is
cited as having liked to read some beautiful passage before
sitting down to work. Emerson seldom began to write without
having read a few pages of Plato. And Dante is not the only poet
Virgil has conducted to the threshold of paradise.
Marcel Proust

Reading now and then
Valentine Cunningham

The act of reading has never been just one thing; and what goes on when we read has never stayed the same for very long. The stuff of reading – reading matter – has changed dramatically over time: from scroll to codex; manuscript to print; hand-print to machine-print; from one-off to mass-production; from the mechanical to the electrical to the electronic; from book to IT screen. And with these technological revolutions the model, or implied, reader inevitably changes. New styles of architecture, as W. H. Auden once said, a change of heart. We might add that with new objects of reading attention, new ways of doing words, there necessarily come new ways of dealing with these words. So a calmly accepting relativism seems indicated as a more or less wise posture? After all, history instructs us, what is the use of whingeing about shifts in technic? Changes come and go. And where are the Luddites now? Simply nowhere.

And, of course, any kind of reading activity is, to some extent, better than none. To have the satisfactions of story, of fiction, for instance, even in the most minimal and simplistic and etiolated of modern forms – comics, comic books, Mills & Boon romances, supermarket and airport novels, say – is to be significantly advantaged in ways that are simply not available to the word-blind. Oral narratives appear to have seriousness, imaginative densities, and to offer audience benefits, but they are generally outstripped for complexity of address and reach, as far as we can tell (and one of the problems of judging some of the best, Beowulf, Homer, Moses, is that we only know them in their edited, improved and written-down versions), by written texts. And when people ask me, as they often do, what I like prospective students of English Literature in my university to have read, I always reply that something – anything, almost – is better than nothing. Above all, I want people to have read and to read, rather than not.

Reading, as such, is liberating and, as they say, empowering. Even at the basest, the most merely instrumental of levels, being able to read is axiomatically better than being illiterate. Dickens invites us in that extraordinarily potent and angry Chapter 16 of *Bleak House* to imagine what it's like to be cut off from the world of signs that urbanised, industrialised modernity comprises, to be like the waif Jo, driven to earn his few daily pence by keeping a bit of London street brushed clean of muck and mire for, he hopes, charitably-inclined pedestrians. 'To shuffle through the streets, unfamiliar with the shapes and in utter darkness as to the meaning, of those mysterious symbols, so abundant over the shops, and the corner of the streets, and on the doors, and in the windows! To see people read, and to see people write, and to see the postman deliver letters, and not to have the least idea of all that language – to be, to every scrap of it, stone blind and dumb!'

The modern urban world – London was then the greatest city on earth – is described by Dickens here as 'the great tee-totum'. London is a game played with words. Modernity belongs to the literate. Power lies in literacy. To be a truly competent individual in the modern world, you need to be able to read. To be unlettered is to be in a primitive, archaic, pre-civilised state, a mere dumb animal. 'Jo, and the other lower animals, get on in the unintelligible mess as they can. It is market-day. The blinded oxen, over-goaded, over-driven, never guided, run into wrong places and are beaten out; and plunge, red-eyed and foaming, at stone walls; and often sorely hurt the innocent, and often sorely hurt themselves. Very like Jo and his order; very, very like!'

But there is, of course, reading and reading. And mere reading, base reading, simple, instrumental reading, does not raise you much above Jo's beast-like level. And what is most striking about the changing nature of modern reading material is how it moves us insistently back to a more and more simplistic, merely instrumental, reading position. We, and it, are progressively dumbed and dumbed-down. We are treated more and more as nearly-Jos, forced increasingly to inhabit a sort of glorified *Reader's Digest* kind of world, the zone of the hand-out, the précis, the ad-man's slogan, the politician's catch-phrase, the government department's brochure, the headline. Public words get progressively baby-like. The lettering up in neon is gargantuan easy-reading stuff. The tabloids' mastheads come in massive print, as if for nursery readers. We're surrounded by baby-words writ large, and simple sentences for the learner reader. Public discourse is made up of little words, short phrases, small paragraphs, brief texts.

It is one of the great ironies of our time that as the means of writing production get more and more sophisticated, modern reading-content gets more and more playschool. Basic reading is driving out what we must call classic reading. And as the old print media get more and more overtaken by their electronic rivals, as the book gives way to the personal computer, the diary to the electronic notepad, the broadsheet to the web site, and the reader with a book in her hand becomes a more and more singular phenomenon and less and less a sign of something automatically regarded as a good thing, and as public libraries become places where computers and not books are housed, it does perhaps behove us (as we used to say before our Americanised spell-check wondered whether we'd got the word right) to at least face the consequences. And the consequences are not just for the business of merely transmitting information, nor even only for education and its assumptions and methods, let alone just for the careers of librarians, but more largely and more pressingly for ourselves – for what we have to call that messy but important business of selfhood.

One learns a lot about reading as it used to be – classic reading – from classic fictions. It's one very arresting feature of old stories, especially canonical texts from the great classic period of modern reading – that is, roughly, from the invention of the modern novel until literary modernism started to unpick the mode – that they keep advertising the benefits and advantages of reading books like themselves. One of classic fiction's commonest of moments is the momentously exemplary scene of reading. Like islanded Robinson Crusoe finding personal hope and salvation in one of the three Bibles he managed to salvage from the wreck of his ship. Or Maggie Tulliver in George Eliot's *The Mill on the Floss* (Book 4, Chapter 3, 'A Voice from the Past'), picking up, in the midst of her own and her family's deep distress brought about by bankruptcy and utter impoverishment, an 'old, clumsy' copy of Thomas à Kempis' *The Imitation of Christ* from the rubbishy slush-pile of books her good friend Bob has bought for her because they're 'cram-full o'print', and having her life transformed as she follows the advice about self-negation in passages marked in faded ink by some long-dead predecessor. Or little Jane Eyre in the opening chapter of Charlotte Brontë's novel, taking refuge in a window seat from her hostile relatives inside the house and from the cold weather outside it, and receiving consolation of sorts from the 'introductory pages' of Bewick's *History of British Birds*. And reading-scenes from classic autobiography endorse the fictional ones; like the encounter with the peasant Huguenot family near Uzès described by André Gide in his *Si le grain ne meurt*, people hearing the Bible read by their grandfather before supper, and whose intelligence and moral dignity seem ascribable to this regular encounter with the word (and, of course, with the Word).

Such scenes of reading – and there are lots more where these came from – keep affirming certain key features of classic reading (features which educationalists no less than writers have come rightly to think of as traditional and once normative). Absolutely noticeable, in the very first place, is that these acts of reading are quiet. Here are people stilled in contemplation, prayerful even, face to face in silence with the words on the page, with words felt to be so important that they merit one's full, absorbed attention, the address of one's whole being. And this quiet reading place is presented as necessary for the growth of the mature person. This is the private space of reflection where a classic Western individuality gets formed. For this is the space where reflection becomes self-reflection. It is, too, extended reflection and self-reflection, because these exemplary books are rather long – as big as the narratives that contain them. And the power of such reading is connected with this extendedness. 'I like those great still books,' Tennyson once confided, and characteristically of the nineteenth-century reader: 'I wish there were a great novel in hundreds of volumes that I might go on and on'. And when the quiet place and time of reading are invaded and abbreviated (as Jane Eyre's are by her brutal fat cousin John Reed) the shock is grievous; the person and her sense of selfhood feel violated. (Jane cuts her head, in fact, on a door jamb, dodging the copy of Bewick that the ironically-named Reed throws at her.)

Noticeable, too, in these scenes, is what post-modernist and deconstructionist criticism has spent the last few decades deploring as logocentrism. Here are encounters, it's felt, with a real, speaking, knowable presence. Here the word is indeed made flesh, given palpable life and presence. The author, not least, is made present. 'Every picture' in the Bewick, Jane informs us, 'tells a story'. But it's the accompanying letter-press which speaks loudest. And like the Voice of God in the Christian concept of His Word, the words of these texts are heard feelingly. It is not surprising to find that the exemplary reading-scene in so many classic fictions is indeed some believer's, or near-believer's encounter with the Judaeo-Christian Scriptures. Robinson Crusoe's reading is much like the reading described by Gide. The Biblicist atmosphere is pervasive – and that is, of course, what logocentrism is all about. Like the character of God who addresses Everyman in the medieval play, and in words which still feature on the endpapers of every book in the Everyman series, the author on these traditional reckonings is expected to appear to the reader, and to go, to walk with him or her. In such acts of reading, the absent author is summoned, as Lazarus was in the Gospel, to come back from the dead, from the distant past, to rise from among the silent signs on the page, and to speak to me, the reader, now in the present; on such a classic view, in the famous words of Milton in the *Areopagitica*, books have 'a life beyond life'. Readers on this plan are what Dickens called (in that extended trope which motors *A Tale of Two Cities*) Resurrection Men. Reading like this is indeed a recalling of the dead to life.

And the result is perceived as educative for the whole self of the reader. Reading like this inducts you into personal and moral growth and seriousness, as well as merely informing you of things. It's an inspiriting that draws its force from its being a kind of sacramentalism. In his lovely and informative book *A History of Reading* (1996), Alberto Manguel nicely illustrates the radically liberating and revolutionarily empowering, but also spiritually enlightening effect of literacy, with reference to a former slave, the 90-year-old Belle Myers Carothers, who told Federal Writers Project interviewers in the 1930s how she'd learned to read from the alphabet bricks of the plantation-owner's child she minded and from a spelling book she found. One day 'I found a hymn-book ... and spelled out "When I Can Read My Title Clear". I was so happy when I saw that I could really read, that I ran around telling all the other slaves'. What, in fact, brought home to the girl-slave her enfranchisement in literacy (Manguel doesn't spell it out) was Isaac Watts's great hymn which offers the promise of Calvinist hope and divinely predestined confidence to the believer who can read the promise aright. 'When I can read my title clear/ To mansions in the skies, / I'll bid farewell to every fear/And wipe my weeping eyes'. To be such a reader, in this context, on this plan, is to feel, and indeed to be graced, for living here and hereafter. The story is a vivid allegory of how the utterly life-enhancing power of the word borrows, or is inflected by, the traditional power of the Word. Logocentrism indeed.

Certainly, reading like this is food for the self. It is material for self-fashioning, for *Bildung*, for self-education, the kind of growth in selfhood that the classic novel, or *Bildungsroman*, goes in for and reveals to classic readers as possibility for their own lives. 'Everyman', the book truly promises, 'I will go with thee, and be thy guide, In thy most need to go by thy side'. 'Here, then, was a secret of life', is what Maggie Tulliver concludes from reading Thomas à Kempis. The *imaginaire* of the person, one's image-repertoire, the images by which one thinks oneself, are provisioned this way. Reading like this is a sort of moral mirror. Here the classic reader acquires the vocabulary for knowing self, and world, and self in the world – receives the 'words to say it'. 'You are like the Roman emperors', Jane Eyre rebukes her terrible cousin: she is able to define him because 'I had read Goldsmith's *History of Rome*'. And so the assumption has been down to modern times. Coleridge finds 'some smack' of himself in Hamlet. Freud bases whole swathes of suggestive understanding of the human upon his classic reading – the Oedipus Complex on Greek tragedy, the Uncanny on E. T. A. Hoffmann's *Der Sandmann*, and so on. Josef Brodsky is enabled to endure in the Gulag by reading Auden's elegy for W. B. Yeats. Arnold Wesker has said he can only imagine experience with the aid of *King Lear* and the Book of Job. Just so, that bookish youth Stephen Dedalus in Joyce's *A Portrait of the Artist as a Young Man* is only able to grasp and identify, to experience truly, his life experiences with the aid of the books he reads –

Alexandre Dumas's *Monte Cristo*, it might be, or Yeats's poems, or the writings of John Henry Newman. 'He heard the choir of voices in the kitchen echoed and multiplied through an endless reverberation of the choirs of endless generations of children and heard in all the echoes an echo also of the recurring note of weariness and pain. All seemed weary of life even before entering it. And he remembered that Newman had heard this note also in the broken lines of Virgil, *giving utterance, like the voice of Nature herself, to that pain and weariness yet hope which has been the experience of her children in every time*'.

Identifying yourself through your reading like this is, of course, a process of entering the 'endless reverberation' of human history, aligning one's own story, the story one tells oneself about one's own history, with the long story of humanity, human-ness, humane-ness.

And it's a long story because such self-knowing through books takes place in that Joycean echo-chamber. Behind all such single acts of reading are many others, arrayed in a long vista of self-knowing through books. It's utterly germane that Joyce is making Dedalus remember the place (Chapter 4, Part 2) in Newman's *Grammar of Assent* (1870) where Newman discusses 'Real Assents' to literature, specifically to Virgil, but also to the classic in general, the tradition of great books, a place where the importance of reading oneself early in life into what Arnold called the best that has been known and thought in the world, is being argued for.

And it is, of course, no accident that such pronounced results should be imagined as coming from books, from codices, from reading dependent upon the act of page-turning (back and forth), not reading reliant upon scrolling with difficulty through a scroll or through the endless, seamless reel of script on your IT screen. That is, from reading built on knowable, checkable sequences, experiences of reading which imply and effect sequentiality of person and life, and thus, too, bring home the consequentiality of actions. The back-and-forth sequential reading that book narratives so readily provide, easily accepts that the moral life implies connectedness, implies, in fact, the existence of the moral 'Law of Consequences' which George Eliot thought of as intrinsic not only to the classic plot of fiction but also to the serious moral life. (And it is, naturally, no accident that Crusoe and Dedalus should have kept diaries, that the exemplary stories of their self-knowing should have assumed the form of the journal, that written monument to the sense of experience necessarily ordered as diurnal sequence, one day before and after another, back to back, side by side, a register of the book-like pages of a life.)

By great contrast, the post-book world is not at all like all this. And it's hard not to think the post-classic reading-scene depleted by its radical differences from what came earlier, not to feel it, in fact, thinned, dis-enriched, disinherited. By its noise, for a start. For the old quiet spaces of reading are now simply blitzed by the noise of the new media, by the sensorama that engulfs us. Even the traditional quiet of the library is disturbed nowadays by the clicking of lap-tops. The new media's modes are all designed to grab attention noisily, to make me a host to loud parasites, to fill my airwaves with noisy interference. (In French, as it happens, radio interference is, happily, *parasite*.) And the electric, electronic invasion deprives me not only of quiet, but of the private choice, the individual selectivity I exercise as a reader of books. We're all of us plonked, willy-nilly, in, as it were, a very loud, densely informative city street, our eyesight hit by clamant, unevadable neon, our ears captive to the throb of passing car stereos. The wireless and the telly are on all the time. We are all bombarded with the bits and bites and bytes of current information. We are flooded with messages. And these signs never come simply, but always multiply. They are crazily synaesthetic, utterly over-determined. There is no song now without a video to go with it; no words – not even in the book sections of the posh newspapers – without a very large picture; no novel without a screen-adaptation coming up (and look at how forcibly prescriptive, as well as skimming and wrenching they usually are).

And this neo-reading-scene is, too, not so much personal as tribal. The post-modern reader is less an individual attending to an individual text than a consuming member of a crowd, of a many in which the self is a blissful syndrome of mass (and, of course, utterly commercial) effect. In the message-consuming throng the I relishes – is supposed, at least, to relish – the blurring of its distinct personal boundaries into the vague vastations of the mass. Here, the dionysiac reigns, the ecstasy (egged on by the electronic world's pharmaceutical cousin Ecstasy) of the Rave, the joyful amoebic corporateness of the rock festival – known, some of them, with great aptness, as Tribal Gatherings. In this Nietzschean scene of reading and being, naturally, anti-logocentrism is the rule. Here, the point of the message, the information, is less substance than style, less reality than appearance. Its substance is the depthlessness welcomed by some post-modernists as the virtue of the great invention of IT-as-commerce, namely video. Meaning by MTV. And what counts in the text of video, or in video-ised textuality, the story in and of video, is certainly not real presences, nor indeed the persons, the characters which are the common goal of the acts of representation going on in books for classic readers. Here are no humans but merely icons, idols. Here, selfhood matters rather as mere fantasy-object (Diana, Marilyn, Gazza), distant objects of desire (tele, telly, presences), Baudrillardian simulacra of the real, virtual personality for the virtual world, electronic substitutes for the old kind of *dramatis personae*. Not Hamlet and Emma, Robinson and Job, Pip and Jane, but quiz-show hosts, weather-girls, speaking-clock voices, stars. Mere images, rather than representations of the real, the human, the personal realium.

And in this world text becomes post- or pre-linear. The bound collection of pages gives way to the loose pile of spreadsheets. What's available online is certainly encyclopedic, but it comes as a highly fragmented field, piecemeal, a montage, or set of montages, a dense and fluent experience of the legible, but a Dada-ist one, a set of surrealist cut-ups, a series of mere cut-and-paste jobs. It's as if our sense of story, and of the human story, had chucked away the achieved maturity of classic realist fiction, connected, linear, sequential, for the less mature, jotty, patchy, spotty status of the old epistolary novel which was a kind of failed experiment in narrative, a fictional siding or branch-line. What characterises, of course, the great democratic field of the Internet and the World Wide Web is precisely freehand jots, random thoughts, amateurishly rambling confessionalism, a neo-epistolariness gone quite mad. And, to be sure, ordered sequence and connectedness of narrative and of concept and person, the great features of classic fiction and classic Western selfhood – of the book, no less – are bound to count for less when, at the touch of just a few buttons, you can swiftly cut and paste everything to somewhere else.

Indeed, what price the word, the written itself, when the push of a button or two can erase the whole lot? Easy go, the message of IT text seems to be, therefore, easy come. Which fits in nicely with the new message explosion's manifest ethos. Too many of our loudly broadcast bits of information, the great rosters of incoming images and noises, are just throwaway stuff, ephemera, never intended to have a shelf-life. Gab in gab out. So, of course, the old central features of the logocentric don't matter so much. Authors – who worries about them? Who cares who, if anyone, wrote that soap? Last year's plots are already old hat. Re-reading a favourite novel was normal; but it's only some kind of camp or kitsch gesture, a pose, if you like watching old soaps. And as for the words that are still left in the frame, in the picture, on the page, on the screen, they simply lack clout. Post-modern words matter less than words once did. So we all get horribly casual about the old questions of verbal point and meaning, accuracy, truth and relevance, as well, incidentally as about all the once carefully attended-to features of writing, grammar, punctuation, spelling, and the like. That pun, that bit of word-play you call a student's attention to, well it might just be some spelling mistake. The copy-editor's careful error-chasing trade is dying out. We all chortle merrily over the *Grauniad*'s errors. Greengrocer's apostrophes, as they used to be called, occur now in the best of families and universities.

Of course classic reading was hard, and still is. As witness all those novels at the beginning of the great modern tradition which register the shock of sequence and consequence and the perils of bookish lineality, and dwell on the sheer physical burden involved in merely keeping the pages turning – like *Tristram Shandy* with its endless pained dodgings and deferrals, or like *Gulliver's Travels*, whose hero clambers about his vast reading step-ladder in Brobdignag to negotiate the near-impossibility of the big book. The reading-scene in classic text after classic text is a place of distress as well as of pleasure, an affair of mistaking as well as useful taking. Reading in *Crime and Punishment*, it might be, or *Sons and Lovers*, or *Don Quixote*, is shown as a frequently error-strewn path. What Maggie Tulliver learns from Thomas à Kempis does, in a way, destroy her. Dostoevsky's Sonia Marmeladov does not bring the criminal Raskolnikov back to the moral life by reading to him from a good book – not even when she reads the story of the Raising of Lazarus from the dead.

But even more dismaying than any sense the tradition might convey of the complexities and elusivenesses of the bookish reading life, has been the way that whole sections of the Literary Academy have recently thrown in the reading towel and that contemporary Literary Theory has connived in afforcing the post-book scenario – deliriously Nietzschean in its hostility to the logocentric, authors, presence, canons, classics, as well as to individual selfhood, 'humanism' and the works of so-called Dead White European Males; shockingly eager, what is more, to dissolve specifically literary study into the looser game of 'media' studies, to collapse all media into 'text', to democratise all utterance as 'literature'. Literary theory has reached a pretty pass when it lacks the means to discriminate between *Bleak House* and some amusing graffito story scratched on the back of a lavatory door, or the extremely similar confessions that pack the Internet; when it fails to define the textual differences between some rock video and *War and Peace*. It's a far too blithe spirit that heedlessly refuses to perceive the consequences of the changes of heart, as we might call them, which follow from new styles of modernist and post-modernist reading even more dramatically than they do from new styles of architecture.

Sense and semblance: the implications of virtuality
Sven Birkerts

There is right now, here, at the Boston Atheneum – a place we might think of as the very cradle of bookishness in this country – an installation by Susan Gamble and Michael Wenyon entitled 'Bibliomancy'. The display is as unadorned and simple as can be. Entering the large, bare exhibition room you see arrayed before you, singly, with wall space in between, 54 holograms of book spines. Approaching to inspect – and, of course, even the non-bibliophile is compelled to do so – you note various things: how the illusionism encompasses the spine and part of the top of each book, with the rest receding into apparent shadow; how the books themselves seem utterly miscellaneous, ranging from *Correspondence General*, Tome 8 of Voltaire to *Pursuing the Whale* by John A. Cook. You stand and look and try to ponder, by and by taking note of the holographic images on the right and left walls – the outside faces of several old-style card catalogue files, a sight every bit as familiar to most of us as that of the assorted spines. You stand a bit longer, waiting for some revelation to break over you, but it never does. At least not the sort that asks a swift intake of breath. But at some moment, likely, you get the point, and then indeed a shiver of displacement may travel through you. Yes, here you are, standing in a barren room, surrounded on all sides by tens of thousands of books, and you are suddenly, courtesy of holographic technology, able to see things at a slight remove, as if, historically speaking, you had just recently turned your back on a way of being and had taken a step away and were casting a last over-the-shoulder glance back.

A few years ago, I wrote an essay called 'The Fate of the Book' in which I tried to sort out the deeper differences between print and electronic-information cultures. The premise, which I still subscribe to, was that we are living through a watershed moment, a monumental transition in which the centuries-old print-on-paper paradigm is very rapidly being shouldered aside by circuit-driven technologies. As the modes are very different in their fundamental nature, it interested me to speculate on some of the possible consequences of such a paradigm shift. I featured them to myself in terms of a set of crucial oppositions. Let me outline them here.

1. *Closure versus open-endedness*. Among many other things, the book has always represented to us the ideal of completion. The fixity of the word imprinted on the page and our awareness of the enormous editorial and institutional pressure behind that fixity, send the message that here is a formulation, an expression, that must be attended to. The array of bound vol-

umes on the library shelves communicates that knowledge and understanding are themselves a kind of structure assembled from these parts.

Screen technologies undo these assumptions implicitly. That a work comes to us by way of a circuit means that we think of it as being open – available – in various ways, whether or not we avail ourselves of those ways. The medium not only allows – it all but cries out for – links, glosses, supplements, and the like. Whatever one reads, and however one reads, it is never with the totality in view. Reading from a screen is like travelling from coast to coast with only adjoining local maps as guides.

2. *Hierarchy versus the levelling of hierarchy*. With print texts, the push to finality, to closure, is also a push for the last word, which is but another way of characterising the struggle for vertical ascendancy. If intellectual culture is seen as the product, or benefit, of book learning, then it is the Darwinian marketplace of ideas that decides which texts will shape our thinking and our values: the age-old battle of the books.

But now substitute screen textuality, put mutability and open-endedness in the place of definitiveness, and it's easy to see that notions of hierarchy will be very hard to sustain. Many, of course, view this enthusiastically and cheer on the erosion of hegemonic authorship. In the theoretically infinite database, all work is present and available – and, in a way, equal. Where discourse is seen to be woven and, technologically speaking, collective, the idea of ranking dissipates. New systems of search and access are already beginning to render the notion of the enclosed work antiquated.

3. *Historical layering versus simultaneity*. The system of print textuality has always promoted the idea of culture as a matter of tradition and succession, with printed works leading back in time like so many footprints. Tracking an idea, an influence, we literally go from newer to older physical texts. The scholar's finger brushes the actual molecules of bygone eras. And historical depth has served us as one of our most powerful metaphors.

Screen technologies work against this supposition. They have the power to transpose the layered recession of texts into a single vast collection of cross-referenced materials. They underwrite the post-modern suspicion of the time-line and the continuous narrative. The picture of history that database and screen unroll is one of webs and trees, a field of relations and connections that submerges any notion of story in a vast informational complexity.

4. *The public space versus the private sphere*. Book reading, whatever its ulterior purposes, has always been essentially private. The medium is opaque. The word signifies against the dead-endedness of the paper, and in the process of signifying it incessantly enforces the awareness that the com-

munication originated in an individual sensibility, that its inscription was founded in privacy. Whatever we read thus, we understand to be a one-to-one transmission – Henry David Thoreau or Roland Barthes to myself. Reading from a screen, by contrast – and I understand that people do not commonly scroll through longer works on a monitor – invokes automatically the circuit system that underwrites all screen transmissions. On a subliminal level the traditional assumptions are all undone. The words on the screen, though very possibly the same as the words on the page, are not felt to dead-end in their transmitting element. Rather, they keep us actively aware of the quasi-public transparency out of which they emerge. Emphasis on 'emerge'. These words are not found in the way that one can thumb forward in a printed text and locate the words one will be reading. No, they appear to arrive, and from a place that carries complex collective associations. To read from a screen – even if one is simply scrolling *Walden* – is to occupy a cognitive environment that is very different from that which we occupy when reading a book.

5. *Expressive versus functional uses of language.* A change in our dominant medium of expression will certainly mean a redefinition of our expressive ideals. The way we use language will change – it is already changing – and literary style will be the obvious casualty. Style is not of the essence in screen-to-screen communication; the very premise of this communication is near-immediacy. The more we are linked up; the more available we are to each other, the less we need to ponder what Flaubert called the *mot juste* or exact word. But the fact is that not all truths can be telegraphed and not all insights can find a home in the declarative sentence. To represent experience as a shaded spectrum, we need the subtle shading instruments of language – which is to say that we need the refinements of verbal style. Without them there is a danger that we could condition ourselves into a kind of low-definition consciousness. We should worry not just about 'dumbing down', but also about the loss of subjective reach.

Certainly there were other oppositions to be contemplated, but I stopped with these first formulations. As with anything that remains unfinished, however, the subliminal psyche continued its worrying process. But what I have found, now that I have returned to the subject, has been a discernible shift of emphasis, or perspective. I note that I am less interested now in enumerating significant differences between the technologies – book and electronic – and more occupied with thinking about the kinds of spaces, or subjective cognitive environments, they create, and how these in some way change our conception of knowledge itself. Another small subject.

The matter does bear thinking about. Book space, print space – that which we occupy as we sit turning pages – even though it varies significantly depending on whether we are reading *Treasure Island* or *Principles of Structural Anthropology*, can still be characterised. Occupying it, we are, or want to be, immersed – which is to say, pledged to a single purpose, refined in our attention. Reading books, we have a clear sense of 'ledge', for the immersions are discontinuous from book to book. We know, if only because it is physically enforced for us by the form of the 'technology', where the book stops and the rest of the world takes up again. Reading a book, translating the signs into the invisibility of apprehension, we hold the shell, the weight and mass of the volume, as an anchor. And does this not, I ask parenthetically, form the basis for a profound, if elusive, analogy. That the book, with its concrete exterior and invisible interior – its body and soul – is like us in some way? Discrete, laden. Don't we say: 'She is a closed book to me', or 'I read him like a book'. An analogy to be pursued, but elsewhere.

The space of electronic information is perceived as bottomless. A track ends not of its own accord, but when one decides to stop following it. There is no clear sense of ledge. Knowledge, or any contents, are not figured as existing in space (on page 68, second volume, third edition) but retraceable only as a set of coordinates, commands. One does not find things again so much as they are recreated – brought back into being – upon demand. I see interesting correspondences here with memory theory, the older views supporting the idea of memories as mental contents somehow held in the mind, newer views proposing that memories are created afresh as prompts elicit combinatory responses. Moreover, screen contents, those representing and serving knowledge, are part of the larger stream of all digitised information, adjacent via keystroke (that is: attention shift) to pornography servers, private and corporate web sites, adjacent to *everything* in a way that the contents of bound volumes simply are not. This adjacency is, of course, merely potential, but the awareness of potentiality has everything to do with how we process information.

With the changing of the processes – the means – of knowledge, do we not also begin to change the definition of what constitutes knowledge?

The transition we are going through is eased, but also complicated somewhat, by the fact that the two processes are operating right now, side by side. Most individuals move from page to screen and back again, shifting between immersed and open-ended modes. We are nothing if not adaptable, as our large-scale acquiescence to computing demonstrates so clearly. But I would argue that the two-track approach is temporary, a consequence of transition, and that a few decades hence most of our transactions – and conditioned reflexes – will serve the screen and not the book. Books will exist, of course, and they will have their special uses, but they will be like those older roads we find everywhere running parallel to the big motor-ways. The dominant knowledge environment, or whatever we choose to call it, will be characterised by fluidity, simultaneity, and hyper-complex relationality; it will be non-authorcentric, non-hierarchical, open to entrance and manipulation – collaborative – significantly unedited, and in its totality, no matter how powerful and sophisticated our search-engines and interfaces become, it will be overwhelming. The user will have to contend with intimations of totality that the book-user has managed to escape; one book does not suggest all books in the way that a branch in the data trail suggests a network of endless branchings. The idea of this totality – exhilarating conceptually – is likely to seem paralysing to individual initiatives of the sort that founded and then sustained our intellectual-cultural life for so long. Attainment is, after all, founded partially in hubris, and nothing is so withering to what someone called 'the desire and pursuit of the whole' as the unbounded vista of what has already been done. Specialisation and teamwork, the game plan of the sciences, will become the procedure of art as well.

But how are we to get at this knowledge question? If we agree, Heisenbergians all, that the regard changes the thing regarded, then certainly we are modifying what we understand knowledge to be as fast as we upgrade the processing power of the microchip. The shift from book to screen may, in its eventual impact upon our sense of what knowledge is – how it matters and what its ends are – be as transformative as the shift from Newtonian to Einsteinian physics.

The datum, the fact, the unit of information was once understood, imagined, as fixed, a point mapped to the world, with knowledge seen as a coherent picture made up of points. The same unit is now configured in space subject to relativity; it is in motion, relational, always part of a function. Is this a more accurate picture of the world, or is it that the world simply keeps changing as we modify the rules of looking? By which I mean that there is no picture of the world that stands free of the process of looking. A contemporary cliché, but one worth remembering. In earlier formulations, when knowing was understood differently, knowledge was something one could possess; now it is a relational process that is forever changing – our attempts at apprehension are variables factored into the function.

We are in transit between the habits of the old and the elusive promise of the new. The transformation is inevitable; the new understanding will prevail. Where will it leave us?

A new knowledge system will naturally mean a change in our subjective sense of ourselves. Human agency, and its aims, are being redefined. From this will surely come, in time, a new sense of what it means to be human.

Is it any accident that we are just now hearing on all sides about Steven Pinker's new theories of mind and language – the marriage of the so-called 'computational model' with the precepts of evolutionary biology: mind as highly sophisticated processing system? Or that we are hearing not just about Dolly the sheep – we've already absorbed that – but also about the demiurgic ambitions of Dr Seed to clone the first human? Nor can it have escaped our notice that *the* word, the buzz concept, of the day is 'virtuality' – that which can perfectly seem without, in fact, being.

The new conversations we are having are suddenly possible not only because of specific advances in the various sciences, but also because we are allowing a new set of assumptions about the human to invade our thinking. Our resistance has, in certain ways, been lowered. People are less in thrall, so it would seem, to an understanding of being as sacred, as originating from and destined for a place beyond the pale of reason. We proceed, increasingly, on the assumption that rational, if highly complex, systems underlie mind, biological being, indeed the universe around us. The speed and power of the computer have begun to erode former intimations of mystery, reducing what had seemed quasi-supernatural to manifestations of mere complexity, potentially comprehensible and reducible. We will fully understand intelligence through reverse engineering, by creating it – so say the high priests of artificial intelligence. And when we have cloned a human being we will in some new way be in possession of the big secret, the platform for so many old notions of deity. Of course, we can only get at many of these former mysteries – mind, DNA – by way of high-speed computation; we can't do it entirely by ourselves. But since we created the computing prosthesis, we accept that its achievements are fully ours.

This assumption of reach and capability – capability so great that we will, and fairly soon, have mapped the entire human genome – now attends all of our endeavours. Just as we know the power of our automobile, even when we creep along at 15 miles per hour, so we are aware of the power of our computers, even if we are merely tracking a simple citation. This sense of potential capability, as I suggested earlier, is now part of our changing cognitive make-up. And having experienced it – the speed of access and the combinatory leverage – we find it ever more difficult to go back to the old technology, even though it surrounds us everywhere. The later you were born, the more likely you are to be affronted by the density and difficulty, the obdurate slowness, of the printed page.

To read a book after working with a mouse is to feel yourself paddling upstream. Upstream: where history resides.

A changed sense of potential, a radical increase, alters the nature of our engagement with the actual. When something has ceased to feel necessary, like the only way, we loosen our connection to it, perhaps allow the slightest increment of dismissiveness to inform our attitude.

The past feels slow and stodgy to us, because that's how people lived before they knew what we know. The condescension implicit in our bemusement, bemusement whipped to a fine froth on every television screen in the land, is a terrible betrayal of origins.

I am often struck by the following paradox: that we celebrate these enormous strides of progress, but it is not as though we have really even begun to exhaust the possibilities of the earlier technology. Content and depth, and understanding, remain largely imprisoned in our pages of print. We never really set them free. We are not really adequate to our radically improved technologies.

I deal with students all the time who carry on their intellectual business seated in front of high-powered computers, but who cannot make their way with any confidence through a relatively straightforward paragraph of literary prose.

One kind of attunement – and aspiration – has been displaced by another. Movement across the vast surface of the grid is favoured over immersion in any of its isolated spaces. Correlatively, the knowledge mode now preferred in our culture is one that combines externality with a sophisticated awareness of interconnectedness. Interiority, subjectivity and the more spiritual resonances are suspect.

As we perfect our lateral sweeps in every direction, flying from node to node, we are also pulling away from language. Language, that is, understood as a process more profound than a mere signal system. We are losing our grip, collectively, on the logic of complex utterance, on syntax; we are abandoning the rhythmic, poetic undercurrents of expression, and losing touch with the etymological variety that has always pointed back towards coinages and, implicitly, the historical perspective.

The near-instantaneous movement of data through circuits has the peculiar effect of charging that data with presentness. The winking cursor is the ledge line, the heartbeat of the present, and whatever words or numbers march across the screen have been recontextualised in the now. The word, formerly static, feels irradiated; it has been changed by its susceptibility to electronic commands.

When we look at the screen, peer into its dimensionless shallows, we locate ourselves in a transpersonal perpetual present – not entirely unlike the time-awareness we experience while watching television. This collective present is different from the subjective present we see – experience – when we look around us. The collective element may start to feel safer for some, more like home. When the pressure of self is no longer strong enough to counter the presence of one's surroundings, then one looks, possibly, to merge that self with others.

History, our sense of the layered past, which was represented so clearly by rows and walls of physical books, changes – our subliminal sense of it changes – when we encounter information streaming left to right across a fixed screen surface. When the understanding, the imagining, of history changes, so must our whole sense of what knowledge is change. We cannot simply take up the old inquiry as if everything else but our means of knowing were the same.

For we are not simply augmenting and speeding up the processes of storage, retrieval, presentation and so on. We are modifying perception. The open vista – an expanse of undisturbed meadow – is not seen in the same way in the era of high-speed travel as it was seen when people got about on foot and horseback. Never mind that the eye takes in the identical distribution of shapes and colours.

We are just now releasing the genie of linkage, of complex referentiality, from the bottle. The assumption in most quarters is that this can only be to the good. How can more and faster ever not be good? More and faster is the mantra of the day, and to question this is to be quaint, if not eventually annoying.

But what if we conceive of knowledge not in terms of quantity – data to be accessed – but think of it rather in terms of a dynamic foreground/background tension, with knowledge always being a function of data in appropriate context?

We have liberated data, but in doing so we have also wreaked havoc upon context, which we might think of as the home for data. We live, in George Trow's memorable phrase, 'in the context of no context'.

A piece of data, of information, only becomes a piece of knowledge when it can be understood as the answer to a question. This is the lesson of Edgar Allen Poe's great story, 'The Purloined Letter'. Poe's detective, Dupin, walks through the same rooms as the other investigators. Lacking a question, which is to say a focused narrative, the stooges could only dismantle the premises in their search for crevices. Dupin understood, as it were, the question to which the letter was the answer and he, therefore, was able to pounce on it.

We have filled the world with untethered information, more by many magnitudes than it held even 50 years ago, but for most of us it has become pointless bric-a-brac. The contents of Citizen Kane's legendary warehouses were searched and inventoried, to no avail. No one knew to look for a sled called Rosebud.

We cannot find answers if we cannot formulate questions; we cannot formulate questions if we cannot grasp context; we cannot grasp context if we try to process more information than our sensoria are equipped to handle.

This is not to say that books themselves do not contain mountains of data, much of it lacking comprehensible contexts. But print culture, through its gradually evolved systems – the standardised formatting of books, the consensual procedures of academia – attained what for some centuries felt like a workable balance. The physicalised text, its location in space, subject to ordering systems, manifested this multiplicity offset by specificity, the enormous terrain contained as by a map. We should not give all this over too easily.

I still do not feel that I've reached it, the root of my doubt. What *is* it that so disturbs me about the idea that the new human knowledge environment will soon enough become electronic? Am I really against complexity, or speed, or epically-increased access? Surely my attachment to book systems is at least, in part, sentimentality. The technology can obviously do a great deal more – isn't it foolish not to let it?

Looking for a way to think about this I suddenly recall the advent, not so terribly long ago, of the pocket calculator. How people argued, then, the pros and cons. 'The instrument will release us from the drudgery of calculation; it will free our minds for more complex mathematical tasks.' 'No, it will destroy in users, in students especially, any deeper understanding of the process, the logic of the calculation. When a square root is a button-tap, then after enough button taps the concept vanishes; it is simply a thing one does.' 'But so what? What does this understanding matter now that we have tools that will do the work? Do we still need to know how to milk a cow or skin a deer?'

So it would go. I sided then with the worriers, and I side with them now in this far more critical matter. The underpinnings of my position are essentially the same. To entrust calculation to a machine, useful as it undeniably is, is also to distance oneself from the cipher system of mathematics and the idea of its intrinsic correspondence to reality; it is to impose the abstraction – the mediation – of a mechanical operation upon the abstraction of the numbers themselves. Understand, as I say this, that I am arguing on behalf of a concept. If I fly, and sometimes I have to, I prefer that the air-traffic controllers do their calculations on computers rather than scratch pads. Still, the point has to be made. Handing over any function – having an accountant to do your taxes (I do); a mechanic to repair your car (I do); a service to maintain your yard (I don't) – removes you to an obvious degree from the reality, the necessity, of that function. It plants you more deeply in that frictionless secondary environment, the apotheosis of which is virtuality. Which may be where we are all headed eventually – into lives mediated at every point, where almost no contact is made – ever – with the myriad functions that were once accepted (and often lamented) as our lot.

But this is a matter for another essay. Here I simply want to make the connection between that removal of self from the fundamental processes and what is likely to be the larger personal and collective consequence of rushing into a new knowledge environment. Basically, we are increasingly entrusting to software the various gathering, sorting and linking operations that we used to perform for ourselves, and which were part of the process of thinking about a subject. We have to ask, not just 'what does software do, and what does mind do?' but 'what should software do, and what should mind do?' I fear that we will preen ourselves on our astonishing conquest of data, even as we ignore the fact that the better part of any knowing is a grasp of the underlying epistemological principles. Half of any knowing is knowing how knowing works. For every decision, every personal initiative we undertake in the realm of information, reaffirms the system of laws that makes knowledge possible and useful.

In this connection, then, we need to address the question of imagination. For there is a serious danger that that capacity, that muscle, will atrophy from lack of use. Imagination is the means by which we create bridges and connections; it is how the self responds to a gap or an absence – it is a way of creating coherence. But it requires, always has, obstacle and deficit. In the seamless world, the world of click and point, the world of proliferating links and synapses, where every line of thought is seen to connect by branching paths to other lines of thought, there is no void to project towards, no gap to fill. Like children growing up with all desires attended to, we submerge ourselves in the universe of surfeit. And that muscle of imagination, trained ancestrally on barren cave walls, on distances and longings, weakens. Like the great muscle of memory in earlier days, it atrophies, perhaps in a few generations to become vestigial.

Dare I push this a notch further? Say that without absence, without intellectual want, without ledges and baffles and barriers to crash against, without being able to formulate the pressing questions that awaken data from potentiality, we may begin to lose our own sense of boundedness, of definition. Distance and difficulty – yes, and slowness – help confer limit; their lack induces us to feel life as a continuous dream – a dream that must, alas, dissolve, for we have not yet schemed a way around mortality. The loss of boundedness is a hallmark of our strange age. We may begin to feel, at first almost imperceptibly, then with an anxious twinge, that we are leaking out into the world around us. When the water is just at body temperature we can't tell any more where the skin ends.

I pull myself back here. I see now that my thoughts have begun to spiral out too far from their original object, this installation of holographic images. Shaking my head, stepping back a few feet, I can make myself see them again for what they are: straightforward unspectacular illusions, static images of what we still find everywhere in the world around us. Books, vessels of thought and creative impulse, no more noble or sacred, any of them, than what they contain. In the wake of dire imaginings comes the exasperated countering voice, telling me, basically, that I must learn to live in the world without worrying quite so much.

Television and literacy
Colin MacCabe

Television is, despite the recent advances of satellite and cable, the most national of media, still anchored in the national news which provides its core of content, as it is in national regulations which provide its political and economic form. If television provides one of the most secure bases for an understanding of the contemporary imagined community of the nation, then the other is provided by the school.[1] If the fact that we are all watching the same news at 10 o'clock provides one axis of the contemporary national community, then the other is the guarantee that all our children are studying the same curriculum. It is surely no accident that our new Blairite government which is trying for a modern, where Thatcher tried for a Victorian, renewal of the nation, has as its twin themes education and its own presentation in the media.

But it must be said that to conjugate television and education together is very difficult, and that is because there are two paradigms which are so well entrenched that no sooner do you mention the words in the same sentence than it is immediately assumed that you are arguing in one discourse or the other, and almost nothing that you can say will persuade people otherwise. I, therefore, want to start this essay with a very brief account of how I, myself, experienced television and education as a pupil nearly 40 years ago in the Britain of the early 1960s, for, at one very basic level, my views on these matters are the same now as they were then and are, perhaps, most easily understood in that historical context. These matters need some glossing because there are few institutions which are so easy to understand in their present form, but whose past forms immediately disappear into national amnesia. Just as it is practically impossible to understand how the French, German and Italian educational systems actually function, unless you have been through them, it is almost impossible to remember how education functioned before Local Management of Schools was introduced, let alone before Crosland's famous circular in 1965. Similarly, the exact division of network channels in other countries is always mysterious, but no more than our own television chanelling before the advent of BBC 2, not to mention after the arrival of Channels 4 and 5. It is the inevitable counterpart of their centrality to contemporary nationhood that it is very difficult to understand the precise ways in which educational paths and television channels interact outside one's immediate time and place. We may globally watch the same sport, consume the same goods, and enjoy the same films, but our sitcoms and our soaps, our news and our current affairs, our exams and our teaching remain national and different.

In Britain in the early 1960s, I enjoyed two excellent educations. Thanks to the Butler Education Act of 1944, I benefited from the national determination that able children should enjoy a grammar-school education and I, therefore, received a thorough grounding in the high cultural tradition. If the classics played a part in this, it was minor beside the place assumed by English literature. The Leavisite revolution which decreed that English literature should assume the culturally central place once occupied by a mixture of classics and Christianity, was an accomplished fact at my own school, even though many of the teachers were Benedictine monks. For my Leavis-trained teachers, television was an excrescence: the most visible evidence of the mass culture which was such a degrading feature of modernity, no responsible parent would allow one in the house. Luckily my parents were irresponsible and through British television of the early 1960s I was exposed to the best contemporary drama, the most informative current affairs programmes and the full range of the arts from pop music to painting and, perhaps most important of all, to situation comedies whose genius sprang from their creative roots in the enormous social revolution of the Second World War.[2] If school and television were held to be separate and, indeed, competing realms by my teachers, they were for me complementary parts of the same process.

Forty years on, it is extraordinary the extent to which television and the school are still held to be separate realms when it is clear that at every level they overlap. And there is no greater key area of this overlap than literacy – the very point where school and television are most opposed in both the bureaucratic and the popular imagination.

There can be few more charged educational debates than those surrounding literacy. On the one hand stand an army of conservatives positive that the traditional skills of reading and writing are declining; on the other, a host of progressives protest that literacy is much more complicated than a simple, technical mastery of reading and writing. This second position is supported by a host of academic work devoted to literacy over the past 20 years, particularly in social history and anthropology. These studies argue that literacy can only really be understood in relation to its social, technical and educational context. Our simple notion which makes literacy a purely technical acquisition of the skills of reading and writing is, itself, an historical product.[3]

In Renaissance England, for example, many more people could read than could write and within reading there was a further distinction in which many more could read print than could manage manuscript. An understanding of these earlier periods is a useful preparation for a comprehension of the current 'crisis in literacy'. Indeed, the huge volume of academic study is itself a complicated response to the contemporary situation. While there seems to be clear evidence that there has been an overall decline in some aspects of reading and writing (a comparison between the tabloids of today and those of 50 years ago reveals a clear decrease in vocabulary and simplification of syntax), the picture is not uniform and doesn't readily admit to the simple distinction literate/illiterate which had been considered adequate since its appearance in the middle of the nineteenth century.

Although little in this area is evident, one might speculate that it is use and interest, rather than teaching methods or moral turpitude, which produce the confused situation today. While reading and a certain amount of writing are as crucial as they have ever been in industrial societies, it is doubtful whether a fully-extended grasp of either is as necessary as it was 30 or 40 years ago. While print retains much of its authority as a source of topical information, television has, since the 1950s, increasingly usurped this role. At a domestic level the ability to write long and fluent letters has undoubtedly been very hard hit by the telephone, and some recent research suggests that for many people the only use for writing, outside the educational system, is the compilation of lists. At the same time, the number of forms of entertainment which do not require command of the written word never ceases to grow. The decision of some car manufacturers to issue their instructions to mechanics as an enormous video pack, rather than as a handbook, might be taken to spell the end of any automatic link between industrialisation and literacy.[4] In a contradictory movement, it is also the case that ever-increasing numbers of people make their living out of writing which is also probably better rewarded than at any other time in history. The tendency of the great media cartels to run from the most popular television, through printed journalism, to the most upmarket publishing, gives some idea of the very complicated ecology in which the printed word both gains and loses power.

Historically, of course, the new and old media are simply seen as opposed. School can be defined as the place where films, television and recorded sound have no place; where the book rules. But it is not at all clear that this historical opposition bears any relation to cultural reality. While you may not need to read and write to watch television, you certainly need to be able to read and write in order to make it. Those who work in the new media are anything but illiterate; the skills of reading and writing are central to all production of this technology.

The technological advances of the last few years make even more apparent that the traditional oppositions between the old and new media are totally inadequate for understanding the world which a young child now encounters. The computer has re-established a central place for the written word on the television screen which used to be entirely devoted to the image – there is even now anecdotal evidence that children are mastering reading and writing in order to get on to the Internet. However, it should not be thought that this re-emergence of writing is equivalent to the printed word. The newest media mix writing, recorded sound and images (both moving and still) in proportions which demand fresh understanding.[5] What is necessary now is to explore the ways in which the new and old media can be integrated in schools to provide the next generation with the necessary skills to produce an economically-productive and politically-enfranchised nation. It must be quite clear that what is being suggested here is not in any way an attempt to minimise the importance of the written word, nor the necessity to improve the standards of basic literacy in this country. There is a crisis in literacy and it would be foolish to ignore it. Because literacy studies are interested in the very complicated set of social relations embodied in reading and writing, there is a tendency for this academic position to simply oppose the conservatives who bemoan the present situation. But to understand that literacy may be declining because it is less central to some aspects of everyday life, must not be equated to acquiescing in this state of affairs. Traditional literacy remains just as central to any full participation in contemporary society as it has ever been. Indeed, the conservatives' moans may underestimate the dangers of the current situation. It seems to me that there is a considerable risk that the information revolution may intensify the division between classes. On the one side there will be those who come from homes who have full access to the new media and who, partly for that reason, will be literate, and on the other will be those who are simply consumers of an ever-more-diverse audiovisual industry and who lose more and more of the functional skills of writing and reading. A particularly dangerous term in this context is that of 'media literacy'. At best, and this is already being very generous, the term is meant to draw attention to the skills that children have in decoding complicated audiovisual forms and which should be built on, rather than ignored in the classroom. But if the term does not include production as well as reception and, even worse, if there is any suggestion that this is equivalent to verbal literacy, then the term simply functions to obscure and legitimate ignorance.

The now pressing question is how these new technologies should be introduced into schools. The fact that the question is pressing should not lead us to underestimate the difficulties of finding answers. It may seem simple to call for computers, camcorders and edit suites in every classroom, but unless there is a detailed and understood pedagogy to go with them, the tools will largely stand unused. Indeed a great deal of the available evidence suggests that this is the fate of the great majority of information technology which is in the classroom.[6]

The most urgent challenge is to determine how the new technologies can be introduced into the classroom, together with pedagogies which will enable those technologies to help children acquire the older and crucial skills of reading and writing. While there is a great deal of experimentation going on in this area, it is remarkable that at least in England there are no developed schemes which link the learning of the skills of recording and editing sound and image with the skills of reading and writing. The British Film Institute and King's College, London, are currently devising teaching schemes which will accomplish this task – which will use the necessity to communicate information through writing in the audiovisual production process as a key element in the learning of basic literacy skills. If it were possible to provide not only theoretical accounts but also, and more importantly, practical models for how traditional literacy and the new media could reach a benign settlement, it would truly mark a new era of education.

It seems very easy in our *fin-de-siècle* era to adopt the pessimistic view. That the new media are destroying old skills and values chimes all too easily with a whole variety of traditional pessimisms from both left and right. But one should not over-eulogise the past. It may well be true that past generations were more literate, but one should be fully aware that this literacy was always a minimal affair. The word itself is a nineteenth-century coinage to describe the divorce of reading and writing from a full knowledge of literature. For Johnson and Milton it would have been impossible to separate the two.[7] The educational reforms of the nineteenth century produced reading and writing as skills separable from a full participation within the cultural heritage of the nation. The new media are not simply turned towards our economic future, they are also one of the key elements in making our cultural past available to the whole nation. A Conservative minister can raise bellows of applause when he tells a Conservative party conference that he wants children taught Shakespeare and not soap opera. The simple fact of the matter is, however, that most children's access to the treasures of our cultural past is initially through television. Each time a Jane Austen or a George Eliot classic is serialised, tens of thousands of copies of the books are sold. The success of *Four Weddings and a Funeral* allowed an ever-canny Faber to sell over 100,000 copies of a special edition of Auden's love poems. These cross-media developments which are the very currency of the modern media industries are to be despised at our peril. Whatever cant is talked about the value of our literary past, it is doubtful whether that past has been available to more than five per cent of the population, and certain that it has not been available to more than ten. If the new media are seriously combined with the old, and the much-derided public-service tradition of British broadcasting makes that a real possibility in the UK, then for the first time it opens up the possibility of making our literary tradition available to the vast majority of the population. Indeed, at one level, this is already happening. Our National Curriculum goes into great detail about the amount of pre-twentieth-century literature that should be studied, and Shakespeare is accorded pride of place at every level of the curriculum. What it is impossible to guess from the official description of this curriculum, but which our researches show to be the case, is that there is no dramatic or narrative fiction of an earlier period now taught in our schools which is not taught without accompanying audio-visual material.[8] The reasons for this are not hard to find – behind appeals to motivation and interest lies the simple, but unacknowledged, fact that these pre-twentieth-century texts are effectively unreadable for most speakers of modern English. The question that must now be answered is whether it is possible to use these audio-visual adaptations to do more than just convey the basic plot; whether it is possible to show the audio-visual text as caught in the same set of fundamental relations: to audience; to institutions; to education as the original literary text, and so make that original literary text readable for the first time. Thus one shows David Lean's *Oliver Twist* not simply to tell the story, but to see how attitudes to the poor, the criminal and the child develop from century to century, and to understand how Lean's film is caught within production relations as constraining and enabling as Dickens's novels first existence in magazine form.

It must be said that the ways in which I am suggesting that the approaches of the new literacy studies and the developments of audio-visual culture should be combined are in no way at the service of a relativist ideology in which any literacy goes. The studies of literacy within anthropology are much animated by a desire to escape the Eurocentrism which is such a distinguishing feature of most of the early study of 'other' and 'primitive' peoples. In particular there has been an effort most tellingly articulated in Lévi-Strauss, to hold in question the unquestioned superiority of writing-based cultures over those which have never developed an alphabet or ideograms. In history, too, much of the most recent interest in the past has been animated by a desire to understand the motives and desires of subaltern classes whose existence bypassed forms of writing. The problem comes when these attitudes and assumptions are translated to contemporary educational problems and are transformed into educational policy. All too often, in practice, they become an acquiescence in under-achievement and illiteracy among the poorest sections of the population. The problem arises when the anthropologist's perspective that any practice of literacy is as good as any other gets transferred to the classroom. While this attitude sits well with the imperatives of anthropological field-work, it does not suit at all the position of the teacher in the classroom. While the anthropologist tries to suspend her own values in an effort to understand those of others, the teacher tries to inculcate the values which are the very purpose of the school. While those values must be responsive to the values of others, it makes no sense at all for them to be considered of no greater worth because, at that point, there would simply be no purpose or point to a school at all.

Here lies the crux of the argument – do we understand the school as a locus of values and knowledge which children are required to learn? No, says the progressive educationalist who, following Rousseau, wishes to free the child from the domination of the teacher and to see the individual develop her full potential with knowledge that proceeds organically from experience. No, agrees the bureaucrat, who is determined that the teacher will not try to deliver outdated knowledge, but will simply manage the organisation of skills which the current state of the economy requires. The fact that although progressive educationalist and modernising bureaucrat agree not one whit as to what the content of education should be (for the progressive everything proceeding from the child's experience and for the bureaucrat everything proceeding from contemporary economic activity), they are absolutely united in their desire to get rid of school and teacher as figures of authority and knowledge. The only voice to be raised against this unholy alliance is the conservative who insists the child should be instructed in the knowledge that has proved valuable to humanity and that teacher and school are there to hand down the wisdom of preceding generations. The weakness of this position is that it tends to ignore both the experience of the individual child and the condition of society generally, and to understand the relationship between teacher and child as one simply of authority and power. It should be noted that on the question of literacy these three positions reverse alliances. While the progressive hesitates to violate the child's mind with the appalling arbitrariness of the written sign and yearns for a new order in which signification will proceed directly from experience, the conservative and the technocrat agree that a basic literacy is the essential bedrock of all education; a functional mastery of writing and reading which ignores all question of content. It is between these three positions that almost all current arguments about schooling and literacy revolve.[9]

The task is to provide a fourth position, one which would found the authority of the school in a description of the teacher/pupil relationship, and which would distinguish it from the relationship of parent and child, of manager and subordinate, of master and servant. It is a relationship characterised in terms of knowledge and in the recognition of a fundamental asymmetry between the teacher and the pupil's relation to that knowledge. The teacher's task is to cultivate the desire for knowledge in the belief that such desire is an economic asset, a political right and an aesthetic good. If we think of teaching from this perspective, it becomes clear that what the teacher is engaged in is the introduction of the child to the order of the social symbolic; of the socially sanctioned organisation of knowledge. Reading and writing are key to this process as the form which has organised our knowledge for 2,500 years. But this century has added extraordinarily to the range of ways in which humanity can record knowledge. The audio-visual forms are now central to our immediate organisation of knowledge and the exact interplay between that immediate organisation and the more complicated dialectic between word and image which sediments into our organisation of the past is something which is still but vaguely understood.

What is certain is that the audio-visual image is absolutely central to the child's organisation of knowledge and that this centrality is still not much appreciated by schools and forms of teaching. On the whole, those who argue for the introduction of these new forms of media see them as introducing a whole new social symbolic. Gunther Kress would be one of the most able proponents of this point of view. His recent book *Before Writing* attempts to provide an account of literacy in which the iconic image becomes the fundamental order of signification, rather than the arbitrary word.[10]

The body of Kress's book is a close and detailed examination of his own children's play and, in particular, their drawing and writing between the ages of three and seven. The book is fascinating as the record of an attentive and intelligent observer's attempt to understand the logics which animate the way in which pre-literate children draw and write. Kress would probably object to the phrase 'pre-literate', as the book is largely an argument to show that children at a very early age have assumptions and theories of meaning and representation which should be built on as they learn to read and write, rather than discarded. Further, Kress argues, these sophisticated theories and practices of meaning are much more in tune with the information society we are becoming than the Gutenberg era of print which is now drawing to a close. As we enter a multi-media world where image, sound and text are combined, we should make sure that we educate our children in ways that develop their abilities, rather than hampering them with outdated notions of the primacy of the printed word.

Much of Kress's local interpretation is brilliant, but the general thesis is sustained by an explicit theory of language which is wrong and an implicit theory of education which ignores all question of resources. Kress is violently opposed to any theory of language which stresses its arbitrary nature. For the small child, and this is the brilliance of Kress's interpretations, all representations are, in fact, motivated. You can understand that these squiggles on the page are a car when you realise that the squiggles are actually approximations at circles, and that the circles represent the wheels which are, for the child, the most significant part of the car. The problem of moving from this to language is that language is, with very few exceptions, made up of unmotivated signs. While a picture of a cat has to look like a cat, the word bears no such relationship to the animal named. Language, therefore, poses an enormous problem for anyone who wishes to locate meaning in individual subjectivity. In order to express our personal views and emotions we have to use a medium which is social and arbitrary. Kress's arguments to get round this verge on the bizarre. Talking about the German word for 'tree', 'Baum', he speculates on its etymological root in the verb 'to bend' and suggests that in the southern steppes of Russia, some 4,000 years ago, the most striking fact about a tree was that it bent in the wind. But even if one were to accept that etymological origins were motivated, this does not escape the arbitrary nature of contemporary language. The only way to make sense of Kress's argument is to view the current state of language as an alienation which in some other society might be overcome. There are hints that this is exactly what Kress does believe, and that what he sees promised by the multi-media future is a world, freed both from the arbitrary and the alphabet, in which pure subjectivities would exchange their emotions in motivated images. Such a Romantic vision would have been all too happily recognised by that doyen of educational progressives, Jean-Jacques Rousseau.

Independent of the question of whether this view is sense or nonsense, and both Freud and Wittgenstein would suggest it is nonsense, it is profoundly dangerous. Access to the multi-media world of the future is controlled in the present by those who have mastered the written language. Kress writes eloquently about the bleakness of the increasingly divided society that we are becoming. An education system which does not place traditional literacy at the centre of its concerns will accentuate these divisions as the world will divide into those who can actively use the new communications technology and those who will merely consume it. It is true that the schools must engage much more actively with the new forms and media, but that engagement must include an emphasis on traditional literacy which remains ever more central to power and authority as it becomes less central to entertainment and leisure. The educational argument which opposes a traditional conception of a single literacy to a more recent conception of many literacies, thus conceals a multitude of intellectual and political arguments. There can be few more pressing questions over the next decade as to how the technologies of information and entertainment enter the classroom and how the relation between new technology and traditional culture is negotiated.

There is a fundamental theoretical dilemma at the heart of my proposals and hypotheses. What I am asserting is that the child will have no access to what I have called the socially symbolic organisation of knowledge unless the audio-visual image is brought centrally into the curriculum. But how will the audio-visual image work its magic – is it that children will bring the critical distance that they have developed while watching the moving image into their contact with another medium with which they are less familiar? Or does that medium itself – the written language – have properties which develop this critical distance in a way that the image with its iconic relation to the referent cannot? On this account, all that the audio-visual image accomplishes in the classroom is that it allows the child easier access to the written language. If I favour the second explanation, it cannot be said that there are absolutely compelling arguments or evidence on one side or the other. What is certain is that writing – in which the speaker and the situation are absent from the moment of communication – insists on a passage through the symbolic which much more clearly involves a moment of personal annihilation, what Freud would have called the experience of castration and what common sense calls losing oneself in another world, than either speech or image. But speech and image are just as firmly articulated within the symbolic and have moments of annihilation just as inextricably bound up in their articulation. The paradox of all knowledge is that its representation of the world never contains the conditions of that representation.

For over 2,500 years, since Socrates first enunciated it in Athens, the crucial goal of Western teaching has been to lead the pupil to herself achieve the position of not knowing – to bring all your knowledge into doubt.[11] It is this that is the final aim of all true education. The first government to find this an unpalatable educational policy was in Athens in the fifth century BC and Socrates was, as a consequence, required to drink hemlock. Even if one may be spared this fate by New Labour, it is nonetheless the case that it is a long way from the education, education, education beloved of Tony Blair in which all knowledge will be delivered by computer and measured arithmetically. While standardised testing is a crucial tool in educational development, the final goal of education, the conclusion of an inter-subjective relationship so that the pupil is a more creative and independent person, is difficult to measure as it would involve tracking all the pupils of a specific teacher and trying to estimate the positive or negative value that the teacher had contributed to each pupil's life.[12] Complicated as this measurement would be, it is the intuitive common sense of films in the *Goodbye, Mr Chips* genre and is also the animating idea behind the Government's recent commercials which emphasised the relationship of teachers to famous individuals.

In talking of the relation between television and literacy, we have immediately been drawn into the most difficult questions of epistemology, as well as the most urgent problems that our society faces. I have sketched what seem to me to be hypothetical solutions to these problems, and I have done so entirely from the perspective of the school – that is I have asked what it is from the perspective of the traditional curriculum that the media can provide. The scale and consequence of the answers may make them sound radical, but I want to stress how conservative is the perspective I have adopted here. It is one linked to traditional conceptions of the public and the national. There is another perspective that could be adopted, both private and non-national, in which it is not education which will harness the media to its traditional goals, but the media which will replace educational provision in the schools. There is no doubt that this is one of the scenarios within the global planning of contemporary capitalism. The growth of universities located within private industries and the explosion of cable channels devoted to learning might make this seem a likely development. And yet all the research which has been done on television and education suggests that while audio-visual material can be very useful when used by a well-trained teacher, and while audio-visual material can be used educationally by someone already educated, it is doubtful whether audio-visual material by itself can teach anybody anything.

This is no surprise to someone who believes that education is fundamentally a transferential relationship. We learn because the teacher is what Lacan called 'a subject supposed to know', a figure who stands in the place of knowledge and from whom we finally learn that we must assume the responsibility for knowledge ourselves. This is what Richard Hoggart calls 'critical literacy'; this is what Matthew Arnold, a century earlier, called 'culture'.

Much of contemporary humanities is concerned with the global and the post-colonial at the expense of the national. This flight into geo-politics is normally accompanied by a corresponding flight from the ethical (too worryingly connected with the subject and the local) into the aesthetic. But in the national education systems and the fundamental ethical problems they pose abide our question. For if the global is to be more than a monologue of the rich, if it is genuinely to become that inclusive conversation which has been a fantasy from Marx to McLuhan, then it will start in the primary schools of the world as children are taught the communication systems of the past and the future in productive juxtaposition.

Notes

1 Benedict Anderson, *Imagined Communities: Reflections on the Origin and Spread of Nationalism* (London, New York: Verso, 1991)

2 For a fuller account of the impact of television in this period see Colin MacCabe, 'Death of a nation: British television in the sixties', *Critical Quarterly* 30:2, 1988, pp. 34–46 .

3 For a good, if slightly ponderous, overview see Harvey S. Graft, *The Labyrinths of Literacy: Reflections on Literacy Past and Present* (Pittsburgh: Pittsburgh University Press, 1995)

4 Colin MacCabe, 'Les Medias: La Mort du livre?' *L'Esprit de L'Europe*, vol. III, ed. Antoine Compagnon and Jacques Seebacher (Paris: Flammarion, 1993), pp. 228–35

5 The great thinker who understood this is the now neglected Marshall McLuhan. Walter J. Ong is also valuable on this topic. Ong's concept of 'secondary orality' to cover forms, like those used by television presenters, which mix the structures of speech and writing is particularly important. McLuhan, Marshall, *Understanding Media: The Extensions of Man* (New York: McGraw-Hill, 1964); Walter J. Ong, *Orality and literacy* (London: Methuen 1982)

6 See Greg Brooks, *Trends in Standards of Literacy in the United Kingdom* (Slough: NFER, 1997); Andrew Goodwyn, *Mother Tongue or Mother Media? The Convergence of Media and Information Technologies and its Impact on Mother Tongue Teaching* (BERA, 1997)

7 Raymond Williams, *Keywords* (London: Fontana, 1983), pp. 183–8

8 The results of the BFI/King's College, London, will be published over the next two years. Early indications can be found in James Learmouth and Mollie Sayer, *A Review of Good Practice in Media Education* (London: BFI, 1996) and Peter Dickson, *A Survey of Media Education* (London: BFI NFER, 1994)

9 For a more extended version of this argument see the debate between Brian Street and Colin MacCabe, in *English in Education*, vol. 314

10 Gunther Kress, *Before Writing: Rethinking the Paths to Literacy* (London and New York: Routledge, 1997) p. 92

11 The vexed question of the relation between Socrates' espousal of ignorance and his confidence in the fundamental knowledge innate in all humans is illuminatingly investigated in Gregory Vlastos, *Socratic Studies* (Cambridge: Cambridge University Press, 1994)

12 M. Chen, 'Television and informal science education: assessing the past, present and future', *Informal Science Learning: What the Research Says About Television, Science Museums and Community-based Projects*, ed. Valerie Crane (Dedham: Research Communications, 1994), pp. 16–59

Hauntings
A. S. Byatt

We now have a complicated and lively image of the learning of language and the development of the brain. We think in terms of networks of neurones, firing and communicating, putting out connections, sending rippling electrical currents, not in simple fixed circuits, but in complex patterns which grow, are reinforced, and die.

The learning of language constructs and is constructed by that web, both in the forms of individual words, and in the forms of syntax and grammar, and beyond that, in the articulate and passionate rhythms of poetry and prose. Both our philosophy and our moral beings are, in a sense, only as good as the strength of those networks. We are animals who learn fastest when we are young and when the network is growing. It is enormously important that all children have the chance to make their webs as strong, and as versatile, as possible.

I know that as a child I, myself, had a shadowy sense of the reinforcing of patterns and connections as I learned things. I loved learning by heart – rules for spellings, grammatical forms – not lists of dates, because these have no structural linguistic use. I missed out entirely on any mathematical mnemonic more complex than multiplication tables. But learning poetry by heart I did experience as the construction of a pattern in my mind of rhythms and rhymes that were both delightful and part of a way of acquiring and preserving both feelings and knowledge. I was upset, when I was a member of the Kingman Committee on the teaching of English language, that the committee members from the teaching profession felt that learning by rote (by heart) was, as one of them said, 'punitive'. It seemed to me to be part of the way the human mind had formed itself since the invention of language. Homer's poetry was learned by heart; his dactyls are beats measured off on the five fingers. The iambic pentameter, I discovered when teaching literature, measures the number of heartbeats in a breath. It is a bodily experience, and should be experienced so. My head is full of pentameters I learned as a child, which are forms of thought and feeling together. I want my children and grandchildren to be able to inherit and enjoy that form of learning, whatever else they may be able to do which I cannot. Children take delight in rhymes and rhythms, from nursery rhymes to rap, from jingles to ballads. Another sad experience I had was watching Terry Eagleton, in a televised discussion with Claude Rawson, refer easily to rhyme as 'an elitist form'. (And no, he did not confine this to the eighteenth-century rhyming couplet.) It isn't. It's ancient and useful and natural almost as breathing.

Another thing that comes naturally to children is the collection of words, as one might collect strange creatures, or marbles. The number of unexpected people who have delightedly recited Beatrix Potter's description of lettuce as 'soporific' to me amazes and delights me. I was much impressed, during the work of Kingman, by hearing Randolph Quirk talk about the primary importance of teaching the extent and range of the enormous vocabulary of the English language – this, he argued, was much more important than grammar, or anything else. It is important to look at words, to savour their histories, the *feel* of their possible combinations, monosyllables with polysyllables, Latinate words with Anglo-Saxon ones, the different kinds of preciseness, descriptive and analytic. Literature is the best, and most surprising way, to do this. Words slot into patterns of thought and vision. Synonyms and metaphors teach us to think both about the inadequacy, and about the rich adequacy, of language.

Another sad experience I had was during a 1970s' reading I gave in a university – a student rose to comment that I had used two words she didn't know, and she thought that was rather elitist of me. I wish she had been simply curious, and asked what they meant. I had not used the words to obfuscate, or distance. I believe in the best and plainest word for the purpose. Behind her political point was an educational imperative that frightens me. It is related to the 1970s' proposal by Ladybird Books to reissue Beatrix Potter with simplified words and pictures; this was aborted by public outcry.

None of these ideas about language is necessarily an argument for teaching the literature of the past. But just as our language is an organic growth, constructed and elaborated by many brains over many millennia, so is our society, and so is our literature. Human beings hand on wisdom from generation to generation, in myths and sayings, in recorded understanding and feeling. Modern literature, modern writing, is haunted by the lively presence of the past – the rhythms of Dickens and Jane Austen are transmuted in the novels of Lawrence Norfolk and Penelope Fitzgerald; Larkin reads and changes Hardy; Shakespeare and the Authorised version of the Bible are pervasive. Indeed, the peculiar deadness of the New Modern Bible is an effect of haunting – it is not really re-translated into modern English, simply 'updated', which destroys the energy of rhythms and makes once-powerful and connected words into inert anachronisms. But the past is, as it has always been, alive in our genes and in our environment. We need to know about, and feel connected to, the dinosaurs. Children still become passionate about Odysseus, King Arthur and the Pied Piper, although recent generations feel less connected to Arthur Ransome's children. Derek Walcott's epic is the continuous and metamorphosed life of Greek myth and Homeric poetry.

A recent (*Paris Review*) questionnaire about Britishness asked me if the British 'laboured under a sense of tradition'. I have recently taken great pleasure in editing *The Oxford Book of English Short Stories*; one of the strengths of these very varied tales from Dickens to Angela Carter is the ease and glee with which they recall and rework past writing, Chaucerian, Shakespearean, Romantic. These stories don't labour, they rollick and indulge. One of the masterpieces is Kipling's *Wireless* in which messages from the dying Keats are picked up in the atmosphere in an experiment with early transmission of radio waves. Kipling's story is about a consumptive chemist's dispenser who transcribes revisions of lines from *St Agnes Eve* and the *Ode to a Nightingale* whilst waiting for the test transmission. The narrative prose is Dickensian, and so is the social comedy, the human observation. But the tentative and beautiful words of the poem are a haunting in every sense – a different and complementary use of what English can do, part of what English people who read know in their hearts about sensuality and the fear of death. In the same way J. G. Ballard's much more modern fantasy about a grounded and lethal cargo of organophosphates on an island depends on Milton's *Paradise Lost* and Shakespeare's *Tempest* for the haunting power of both its strangeness and its mythical universality. Keats, Shakespeare and Milton gave us visions of the nature of things, and we can make our own metamorphoses of these visions as well as adding new, unknown things, including radio and organophosphates. A myth gains power from every repetition; it is not rubbed away like an image on a coin. Great literary images, word patterns, characters and scenes have the same sort of life. When I did A Levels, I had the great good luck to have both *Aeneid IV* and *Paradise Lost IX* and *X* as set texts, which gave me a form for imagining European myths of creation and death at once. And I had Thomas Mann's *Tonio Kröger* in German which gave me an example of the artist-myth and of the use of rhythmic repetition in prose which I'm still learning from.

I am aware of the power of counter-arguments. I have heard children, my own included, complaining that texts they are being taught are not *relevant*, to them personally, to their lives, to the world they live in. We could argue that what is now seen as immediately 'relevant' often seems thin and unsatisfactory a year or two on. There is the danger of young people rejecting what their elders see as 'relevant' on principle. I remember my own daughter's wrath at being taught *Northanger Abbey* exclusively in terms of its relevance to the modern teenager. But works from the past do not all live for ever, and some of the more subtle ones are not best understood by teenagers in classroom situations. I also remember being bored by almost all the pastoral texts I was offered – I hated *Silas Marner* when I was 11 years old, and never loved *As You Like It*, which I was taught when far too unsophisticated, nor W. H. Hudson's slow musings on Salisbury Plain. What I wanted, what I needed, were images of power and terror and beauty and strangeness. I remember suggesting to one daughter's English teacher that the GCSE class should study *King Lear*. She said, which was true, that there was so much she could only tell them at A Level. Nevertheless, I said, the ones who would not do English A Level needed their one Shakespeare to matter to them. They could all think about the battle of old and young, about cruelty and despair. They needed to. The class studied *Lear* and the teacher said it worked wonderfully. My mother always taught *Macbeth* and *Julius Caesar* to rebellious teenage boys. You could teach Graves's love poems, or the Sonnets, but I am not sure about Wordsworth's more ruminative passages. People read less, now, and they read more slowly. The literature they meet must be alive, must be fiercely alive, or there's no point and they're deprived.

This raises the idea of the Canon. I accept George Steiner's useful distinction between a canon and a syllabus – a canon is the literature that goes on living because the living writers keep it alive by learning from it, using it, echoing and re-presenting it, measuring by it. A syllabus is a political construction, based on a pedagogic idea of what students 'ought' to know, for reasons intellectual, personal or social. Canons will look after themselves, to a certain extent. Syllabuses can be useful, inspired, restrictive, or dangerous, depending on the ideas and energies that inform them. When I was young, Dr Leavis's followers were teaching syllabuses of literature that they believed to be good criticisms of life. Now we have egalitarian cultural studies, and the idea that all texts are equal before cultural analysis, which is interesting, but not entirely adequate if you happen to believe in great writing, or real wisdom, as do writers as opposed to students of culture. (Both have their own, and sometimes they overlap.)

One of the things that distinguishes literature from useful writing on society or gender or race is, oddly, the very primitive pleasure principle, which is an essential part of recognising the Arnoldian best words in the best order. Lionel Trilling, in his brilliant discussion of the Snow–Leavis controversy about the Two Cultures, said that both antagonists were puritans, who did not allow for the aspect of art which was pointless and delightful, like the performance of a tightrope walker on a high wire. Literature that stays alive continues to give that sort of pleasure – though I am not saying that it need be immediately available, like candy-floss melting on the tongue. Its presence can be sensed before it is located and experienced. I remember saying, as a child, that I hated Hans Andersen, and knowing, at a deeper level, that he had me hooked, that I could never forget his tales, nor his images. I wrote essay after essay, at 17, on the dramatic superiority of Donne's religious poems over Herbert's, and all the time I knew, some-where inside myself, that the time was coming – maybe years away – when I would care more for Herbert. I even knew how it would happen – I would learn to recognise what even then I called 'achieved simplicity' because I would have read enough to see both how difficult it was, and to have a way of understanding how it was done. You do understand, even at 17, what you don't understand. And what was in store for me, 10 or 15 years on, was the pleasure of recognising the simplicity – of fitting it, indeed, into a pattern of simplicities, achieved and failed, held in the network of memo-ries in my brain.

Pleasure can be deferred and worked for, and so can understanding. One of the great functions of literature for the young is to give them models of life which both deepen the experience they have and suggest, explore, ranges of experience they don't have. There is a place for the study of the immediate world and language of the contemporary culture, but there is also an abiding human need to look outwards at the unknown, backwards at history, inwards at the not recognised. There is a place for spontaneous words, improvised scenarios about depression, but there is a need also for poems like Coleridge's *Dejection Ode* which give a form and a rhythm to despair. There is a place for thinking about what is so good about Adrian Mole or Terry Pratchett, though I suspect that those who teach the things that young people read spontaneously for pleasure put that pleasure at risk. Waugh is funny, too, and Dickens is funny, and their humour is accessible. Sue Arnold and Pratchett are part of traditions that include Chaucer and Shakespeare. Students remember their encounters with great texts as they remember their encounters with great teachers.

Our brains are networks of connections that flash and go still, lie dor-mant. So is our language, and both are privately our own, and quite unable to function without being connected to the general community. When my writing is going well I do have a sense of 'the language' making itself, con-structing shapes and finding forms of thought which are already there to be found. This is nothing, or little, to do with recent theories of language as an arbitrary closed system, with no necessary relation to the outside world, a system that speaks to us, and over which we have little or no control.

It doesn't feel like that. It feels more like a musical instrument picking up rhythms and making sounds that are there, and possible, but good only because of assiduous practice and delighted extensions of technique. Another recurrent depressing experience I have is encountering amateur writers, or writing groups, who say they 'don't read' contemporary writing, still less the writing of the past, in case they contaminate their originality with derivative phrases and ideas. What happens to such writers is exactly the opposite – they produce banal stories, verses like greetings cards mottoes, and *all resembling each other*, because the experience of language and thought they have to draw on is impoverished. We owe our children experience of our language that is delightful, varied, shocking, profound, powerful. We need to start when they are very young, giving them rhythms and words, and we need to go on, with things that are urgently alive, complex and not easy. Not because of a conventional piety towards a vague 'heritage', but because life and energy are inherited and shared before they are transmitted to the next generation.

Love of reading
Doris Lessing

When you meet people who love to read, love literature, it usually turns out that their parents read to them and told them stories, or you'll hear 'I was so lucky, my teacher loved books and I caught the passion from her'. It is usually, but not always, her. Busy parents park their children in front of a television and think that they will get their quota of stories, but quite apart from the crudeness of imagery in most children's fare, what is seen is not the same as what is listened to. One teaches the brain passivity, and there are many who now believe that our brains have been physically damaged by television, and that a general 'dumbing down' is the result of this damage. The other involves imagination, memory, and the secret dreams of a child. There is no more potent witchcraft than 'Tell us a story ...' and then, 'Once upon a time ...' and in later life often the brightest of childhood memories are of sitting very close to a parent, being read to, or, if parents are able to invent, 'There was once a little girl who, oddly enough, had the same name as you ...', or 'A boy called ...'.

People who are not read to, or told stories, tend to inflict the same deprivation on their children. There is now at least one generation of parents and children who have been taught to consider reading of no importance. This is a new phenomenon. At any time up to about 40 years ago, that reading was the best part of education was taken for granted. There was something called a 'cultivated person' who had the Greeks and Romans as a foundation, the classics of his or her own country, the major books of Europe, and perhaps a book or two from the East. Not to mention the Bible, whose glorious and thundering prose was once part of every child's experience and which influenced so much of our literature. But it has fallen silent. This definition does not entirely exclude the working class, for they aspired to books, as the Working Men's libraries and institutes confirm; and novels from the past describe poor people proud of treasured books. This 'cultivated person' is a European definition, but other cultures had – in some parts still have – story telling not merely as entertainment, but as part of education. Marianne Ba (Nigeria) described in her novel *Too Long a Letter* how a girl is sent to her grandmother to be educated by tales imparting morality, the history of her clan and tribe, and proper social behaviour. One way and another, literature, story telling, has been valued. Until recently. A useful book, *The History of Reading* by Alberto Manguel, takes us back to classical times, covering the centuries in between. It could be used by teachers to remind young people of a heritage they have forgotten to value.

'Reading maketh a full man' – and even woman; and surely the task of educators is to remind people what Bacon's exhortation meant. There is a phenomenon now, a person who could be described as an educated barbarian, who may have been at school for 20 or 25 years, has done brilliantly but who has read nothing – knows no history – and is ignorant about anything outside his or her speciality. It is a bizarre experience, challenging any idea one has held about education – particularly when you are with such a person and find yourself having to simplify vocabulary, while you observe blank looks on hearing unfamiliar words like Patagonia, or Goethe. (The great Indian writer Nirad Chauduri, observing that it is now necessary to add, even in *The Times*, after Goethe's name, 'the German poet and thinker', remarked that this proves that Britain is sinking into barbarism.) The trouble is, these new barbarians have no idea how ignorant they are, or how they would have been seen by their predecessors. Some of them are teachers. We have to face the fact that there are many who read nothing apart from the books on the syllabus; have never read for pleasure; and cannot pass on an enthusiasm, let alone love, for their subject.

Perhaps we may usefully remind the young of Jane Austen's famous defence of the novel in *Northanger Abbey*, '... some work in which the greatest powers of the mind are displayed, in which the most thorough knowledge of human nature, the happiest delineation of its varieties, the liveliest effusions of wit and humour are conveyed in the best chosen language'. Or D. H. Lawrence, 'The novel is a perfect medium for revealing to us the changing rainbow of our living relationships'. Or Carlyle, 'The true education is a good library'.

One aspect of the novel is consistently undervalued: it is the amount of information you get, even from bad novels. There are the delights of good story telling, craft, language, that intimate communication, like none other, between author and reader; and then there is information. The novel, in its four centuries or so of existence, has been a kind of parallel education, continually introducing us to our own and others' history, to new cultures, subcultures, places in the world that otherwise we would know nothing about, new ways of thinking – for instance, recently, the women's movement, black people, formerly suppressed and colonised people. The clearest example of the novel as informer is the pre-revolutionary Russian novel. We know everything about it from the great novelists and playwrights. Proust's novel is like a map of that time and that place, France before the First World War, set so firmly in its context – the army, medicine, religion, fashion, food, aesthetics, music, painting, theatre and changing ideas and tastes. If we want to know about the Dreyfus case, there it is, in Proust.

How did the ancient world see itself? Herodotus. Rural life in nineteenth-century England? Hardy. This hinterland of knowledge, information, reference, is lacking in people who do not read.

The new attitude to reading is a direct result of superfluity – if we do not want to acknowledge that our brains have been at least altered, if not hurt, by television. We are bombarded by a thousand ever louder, stronger sensations, and demand ever more powerful stimuli, and the quiet voices of literature find it harder to make themselves heard. If we want to see what we were so recently like, then it is to be found in the Third World, where people hunger for books, seeing them as a key to real education, and respect them as we did so recently. I know a well-known writer in Zimbabwe who taught himself to read from labels on bottles, and stole books to educate himself. In a certain deprived area in the bush, without a proper school or even a telephone, let alone television, a village was supplied with boxes of 40 books. A letter from there read: 'We cannot live without water. Books are our water. We sip from this spring.' Who knows what kind of people may result from these books in a library which is a shelf under a tree. Already there are reading circles, civic circles, adult literacy classes.

We underestimate the effect of slight or single influences on children. Two men, working-class, whose parents took them to Sadlers Wells children's concerts – one man now runs a major music programme for children; the other claims his life was transformed. A single visit to a museum, a concert, a play, a musical, may fire the imagination in ways that only become apparent later. Parents who complain their children get bored so quickly haven't grasped this point that a child embraces a new experience with a total meshing of imagination and need and soon seizes the essence of it, while the need to learn has already moved on to a new source. The parents' complaint really means that they want to inculcate the virtue of perseverance; and I remember dismaying my parents – 'You never stick at anything ...' – but to this day there are skills in my fingers and abilities that are the result of a week or so's enthusiasm.

It is a wide range of experience that children need, and this means that books, literature, libraries, should be seen as treasure-houses of opportunity and pleasure, full of surprises and paths leading to whole worlds of delight, and never a sort of agenda, or requirement of the adult world.

Reading to make us glad
Roy Hattersley

Reading was meant to make us glad – and ought not to be described and discussed as if it were, like good manners and clean shoes, essential to the prospect of employment and the hope of promotion. It is literacy – the power to understand the instruction on the job application form and the ability to recognise the name on the door of the interview room – which is essential to success in the modern labour market. But literacy is only the beginning – the first step towards one of the great pleasures of life, as well as a warm welcome at the Job Centre. Literacy is a necessity; reading is (or ought to be) the most universal and easily accessible of pleasures. As the new centralised schools curriculum increasingly regiments the teaching of English, it is important not to confuse the pleasure with the necessity. Future generations must not grow up to believe that reading, like paying taxes, is an unpleasant obligation to be kept to the absolute minimum.

Some of us are readers by instinct and upbringing. Our enthusiasm is no more virtuous than the possession of any other attribute which is the product of heredity and environment. In fact, we were plain lucky. Thanks to my parents – who read aloud to each other long before they read to me – I assumed that every semi-detached suburban house had pots in the kitchen and books in what we called 'the front room'. Perhaps, more important in its influence on my infant character was the weekly foraging expedition to the Hillsborough branch of Sheffield City Libraries.

We always called the Hillsborough branch 'the library', as if there was only one in the world, and our visits were always on Thursday evening. The regularity with which we walked the couple of miles owed as much to my mother's thrift as to her voracious reading habits. She was determined not to pay the penny fine on 'overdue' books. The choice of date was equally prosaic. Thursday was my father's pay-day – and, therefore, a celebration in itself. So, off we went as soon as we had finished tea, anxious to give ourselves a good hour in front of the shelves before the library closed at 8 o'clock.

I was not simply infected by my parents enthusiasm, I was consciously brainwashed into the enjoyment of a habit which they hoped would help me to achieve their ambition – the appointment as history master in a grammar school. They worked hard to make me like what is now, no doubt, described as the 'reading experience'. Their technique required a great deal of forbearance and self-restraint. They wanted me to read what they regarded as the classics. And, given the chance, they read to me what they hoped would soon become my own choice. I recall one sickly December when, *A Christmas Carol* being finished, my father solemnly worked our way through all of Dickens's other Christmas stories. But, at the library, I was allowed to make up my own mind. That was, I think, part of a conscious effort to make it all seem fun. I am not sure what my mother chose for me in the early days when we went, hand in hand, into the children's annex, but when I was allowed to go alone – while my parents made their choices in the real library next door – the books I brought home were examined out of interest, not suspicion about the habits I was forming. There was surprise that I found Richmal Crompton's *William* tedious and (I now realise) regret that I became a *Biggles* devotee. But they took the view that reading anything, or at least anything that was in 'the library', was better than not reading at all.

I now hold that view in its most extreme form. Any reading – any reading at all – is better than never running the eye along a line of type. Last year, when I advanced this view at a Book Trust seminar, I was asked if I included the *Sun* in my better-than-nothing theory. I admit to pausing for careful thought before I answered, but in the end I said a faltering, 'Yes'. It remains my view; there is just a chance that one thing may lead to another and that a taste for tabloid scandal could develop into a passion to read about the political peccadilloes that Trollope described in the '*Palliser*' novels. But even if that is a rare blessing, the process of reading is, in itself, a benison. What is absolutely certain is that we all have to begin somewhere and few of us start with *Finnegans Wake*.

Reading is habit-forming and it is easy enough to become addicted – once the first glorious step has been taken. Reading can be enjoyed in almost all circumstances. It is the best sort of escapism, providing as it does, company for lonely readers and solitude for those who want protection from the world around them. For two weeks one summer, I sat each morning in the canteen of the Brightside and Carbrook Cooperative Society Dairy and waited to be told which absentee milkman I was to replace. I read *Brideshead Revisited* while I was waiting. It is difficult to think of a novel more inappropriate to my surroundings. But the smell of sour milk and rancid orange juice – not to mention my daily bacon sandwich – did not come between me and Charles Ryder. Thank God, I thought, for reading.

The appeal seems to me to be at least potentially universal – something for everyone as long as they sit back and enjoy it. In the train or bus, bed or bath, beach or park – not to mention sitting comfortably at home – all the reader has to do is turn the pages and absorb the words.   H. L.

Mencken wrote that if the petrol lighter had been developed first, the discovery of the match would have been the sensation of the age. Something very similar might be said about the relationship between books and television. Who wants ready-made images, pre-packaged in a studio, when it is possible to read the descriptions of character and background and then create the picture of your choice inside your head?

Not that readers should regard television or the revolution in information technology as the book's natural enemy. Television – like the Internet and the whole information highway – is an irresistible part of real progress, destined, if properly used, to improve all our lives. And to argue for reading as if television is for idiots and e-mail for androids is to lose the battle for books before it begins. Reading is not part of a better past, but it can help provide a more satisfying future. It needs to make every new electronic invention an ally not an enemy.

Once upon a time, it was the cinema that was going to put libraries out of business. It did not happen. Indeed, it often had the reverse effect. I borrowed a copy of *Great Expectations* after seeing John Mills as Pip in my local picture-palace, and actually bought a copy of *Anna Karenina* after falling in love with Vivien Leigh in the title role. Thirty years later, after watching *Anglo-Saxon Attitudes* on television I returned to a novel which I had heartily disliked when I first read it. Older and wiser I thought it wonderful. In the weeks that followed the BBC serialisation more copies of *Pride and Prejudice* were sold than in the previous 10 years. And do not tell me that few of them were ever opened. We readers should not be priggish about our greatest pleasure. We must not portray it as a superior pastime which is enjoyed by an intellectual elite that does not know the difference between *Blind Date* and *Bruce's Full House*. Reading can be a universal joy as long as we remember the basic principle – it was made to make us glad.

What you reading for?
Jeremy Treglown

The American comedian Bill Hicks used to do a sketch about trying to read a book in a waffle house. The first reaction – before the other customers had a chance to build up a head of scorn and outright hostility – was the waitress's simple bafflement: 'What you reading for?'

Defending the not strictly necessary has always been a problem. Sir Philip Sidney did his best for literature in the teeth of Elizabethan Puritanism ('What you reading ungodly lies for?') by arguing ingeniously that imaginative writing combines the moral improvement of otherwise over-abstract philosophy with the concreteness of (in itself morally defective) history. But he was honest enough – writer enough – to insist that one of its points is sheer pleasure: 'a tale which holdeth children from play, and old men from the chimney corner'.

Proponents of the value of reading mustn't forget about enjoyment. Some harm has been done to the pleasure-based case, though, by the kind of postmodernist criticism which, in rightly asserting that literature doesn't have to refer outside itself – that it can emulate the purity of music or abstract painting – has given the impression that it's always wrong for readers to look for moral or political meanings in a work, or for the illusion of being taken into a world which, though quite different from their own, is somehow convincing and comprehensible. Yet these are among the personal and social needs which literature has always helped to satisfy.

Of course, contemporary Western philosophical questions about the existence of objective reality, moral absolutes and the possibility of communication itself have stimulated authors in ways that have produced brilliant work. Think of Italo Calvino, Milan Kundera, Julian Barnes. There may have been losses. If you want to read a contemporary George Eliot – a living writer who takes you into a familiar social world and uses her portrayal of it to communicate substantial moral imperatives – you'll have difficulty finding one who's much good. But then, George Eliot herself is still in print; she's alive in that very important sense. And meanwhile, some contemporary authors have been producing work which offers insights of kinds which hers couldn't have, into societies and belief systems which she hadn't encountered, as well as moral questions she was fortunate enough not to have had to face.

You would think that the cultural diversity of recent writing was familiar enough, but I was made to doubt this by the reaction to the Booker Prize in 1991, when I chaired the panel of judges. The shortlist, which consisted of

Martin Amis's *Time's Arrow*, Roddy Doyle's *The Van*, Rohinton Mistry's *Such a Long Journey*, Timothy Mo's *The Redundancy of Courage*, Ben Okri's *The Famished Road* (the eventual winner) and William Trevor's *Reading Turgenev*, was criticised for leaving out – what? Not, as most of the judges undauntedly anticipated, any novel by a woman – it was the year of Angela Carter's *Wise Children*, as well as books by Anita Brookner, Margaret Forster, Maggie Gee, Rumer Godden, Penelope Lively and Jane Rogers – but novels set in the UK. This, almost 400 years after Shakespeare had set three of his greatest plays in Denmark, Cyprus and Bohemia. (What was wrong with Warwickshire?)

Like Shakespeare and his contemporaries, today's writers have famously responded to, and helped others to assimilate and enjoy, a period of unprecedented international mobility. No one even semi-conscious who has recently visited a British city could suppose that Bombay, where Mistry's book is set, or a Nigerian village, the locale of *The Famished Road*, is less immediate to the imaginations of readers here than Barchester. And if strictly GB-plate settings are what you want, writers like Hanif Kureishi and Meera Syal surely give at least as good a sense of what things are like for many people in Britain now as Joanna Trollope, let alone Anthony Trollope.

Yet by the time the 'Buy British Backgrounds' line of attack on the 1991 Booker shortlist had been around for a week, one prominent Labour politician had taken it into his head that it was the authors, rather than the settings of their books, that were all foreign. This kind of chauvinism matters for all sorts of reasons. One is the ignorance it displays of the impact which writers have had in helping to create, as well as to tell, one of the great success stories of post-Second World War Britain: the way in which, despite setbacks, a once-powerful but provincial, snobbish and xenophobic little island in north-west Europe was, within 50 years, turned into a surprisingly harmonious multi-racial society. But it isn't only in terms of multiculturalism that contemporary writers have opened new terrain to their readers. If we understand more than our grandparents did about the intricacies of gender and sexuality, it's partly because of the work of novelists. And despite Theodor Adorno's famous claim that after the Holocaust, imaginative writing was impossible, it is novelists and poets, more than historians, who have helped us to grasp the reality of the Nazi genocide – as also of Stalin's Gulag and the nuclear immolation of Hiroshima. No one supposes that explorations like these, crucial though they are, represent the only worthwhile kinds of new writing, or that books must always be 'for' something. But when the uses of literature in moral, social and historical education are being downplayed at precisely the same time as 'citizenship' is being advocated as a classroom subject, it can seem that some old cultural bridges need to be rebuilt.

In the present amnesiac climate, the very fact that ideas about the social usefulness of literature have been around for a long time militates against them. Plenty of people believe that film, television and interactive computer games have overtaken the printed word. Granted, successful movies as diverse as *Schindler's List*, *Orlando*, *The English Patient* and *Jackie Brown* (not to speak of adaptations of almost the complete works of Jane Austen and Henry James) began as novels. Granted, too, that even writers whose imaginations have been stimulated by computer technology, such as Iain Banks, choose prose fiction as their medium. Still, these are transitional phenomena, it's argued – little less quaint than Penelope Fitzgerald's writing her books with a pen. The next generation will see the end of all that.

Wrong. You don't have to be blind to the immense power of audio-visual technology to know that the written word will always offer unique imaginative and intellectual scope to those who have the means to exploit it. This isn't only, though it is partly, a matter of practicality – try using a laptop on a beach – or even of durability: the twin miracles by which a many-hundred-year-old book, never reprinted, can be found in the British Library in full working order, or – like Ovid's *Metamorphoses* in Ted Hughes's version – can get on to the bestseller lists. There are all sorts of ways of transmitting words, but for certain degrees of associative power and communicative density – poetry is the purest example, with 'literary' fiction close behind – writing and reading are indispensable.

The trouble is that like all forms of communication, they have to be learned. Arguments against 'elitism', in this connection, are attacks not only on value but on skill. They are also inconsistent with support for excellence in other areas, such as sport and technology. But forces other than 'dumbing down' – other than mere dumbness, even – have been helping to drive educational policy. Commercial agendas are something to do with it, or so it can seem when Bill Gates is encouraged to cosy up to policy-makers but music teachers are brushed aside. Computing and sport are bigger businesses than books and musical instruments and our schools are duly positioned to deliver entire generations of eager customers. Questioning such agendas is, of course, one of the things which literature encourages readers to do, while also giving them endless enjoyment. It's what we read it for. No wonder governments don't seem keen to invest enough in it.

Critical Literacy and Creative Reading
Richard Hoggart

Under the present Government, two areas of educational activity are rightly receiving special attention: literacy and reading. Obviously, the two are twinned – literacy is fundamental, the essential gateway, the starter tool; without it we cannot read at all. Yet even with it, when we are officially passed as 'literate', we may be able to read only in the barest sense. We may understand the dictionary meaning of an approved number of words; we may be able to interpret what those words say when they are strung together in sentences and paragraphs, but only so long as the words are not very polysyllabic or abstract or heavy with imaginative meaning – the words in a well-presented guide to simple cookery, say, or to driving a car, or to putting together a plain piece of do-it-yourself equipment.

All such gains are helpful and a justification of the present drive for literacy, whether that is labelled 'basic' or 'initial' or 'vocational'. They take us so far; are the absolute minimum needed in any modern society, and not very demanding. Which makes it all the more necessary, as this Government is insisting, that at the age of 11 many more than the present two out of three pupils should reach Level 4 at Key Stage 2 of the National Curriculum.

From basic literacy to Critical Literacy

But, and it is an enormous 'but', a definition of literacy which stops at Stage 4 is inadequate for effective adult life in developed, open, commercial societies such as ours. It would be inadequate even for closed authoritarian societies, too.

The ruling bodies in all types of society must create, in the fashionable jargon, their 'hegemonies'; must create a sense that their kind of society is self-sufficient and self-justified. They all do that by persuasion, and preeminently by persuasion through language. But the kinds of persuasion differ. In authoritarian societies the persuasion is collective and socially insistent; we are incessantly required to accept that this is the best of all forms of society and so urged to join the body of citizens in going the way this particular world is going, by acts of public belonging.

In open, 'democratic' societies, too, we are invited all the time to approve of and join a sort of collectivity, but now of what are presented as congeries of free, self-valuing peer groups, chiefly in buying much the same sort of thing, or doing the same sort of thing, or being amused by similar things. We are not so much asked to join the collective as a self-justifying political end in itself, but to appear to decide to become a part, each by an individual act of choice (or what is made to look like one), of our peer groups and their group tastes. The difference is important and decides the different tones of voice with which in each type of society we will be approached.

We are approached, then, in a society such as ours, by a multitude of voices, very few explicitly directional, almost all peer-group-plus-individual aimed, would-be persuasive and occasionally simply informative. By this immensely elaborate, continuing, successive process do mass, highly-developed, non-authoritarian societies exist and keep on existing. In that process the primary engines are the complex and endlessly developing techniques for mass communication. There is no point in doing more than mention here their manifest value in all sorts of ways. Air travel, rail travel, road travel, the transmission of essential knowledge of all kinds from medicine to weather patterns and beyond; without modern mass communications technology all such operations would seize up, and we would be the poorer for it.

It may be said that the argument so far has been almost entirely that modern societies must go beyond initial literacy, must add to that base all the information and knowledge essential to coping adequately with many aspects of life today. That is true but still does not go far enough. These are also the societies of competitive-commodity-promoting and that puts a very different spin on the processes just described. Plainly informative voices are subordinate not to the bullying but to the cooing and wooing, the deceptive and corner-cutting, the selectively suggestive, so that more goods should be sold, yesterday's goods discarded in favour of today's; and so, too, yesterday's habits, prejudices and notions.

This encourages and creates new forms of two types of work: public relations and advertising. For reasons which will soon become clear, I refrain from calling them 'professions'. They have both, especially since the last war, seen major growth. But the massed ranks of public relations operators and advertising experts are concentrated very much more on persuasion to buy what it is in someone else's financial or influence-gaining interest to encourage us to buy, than in objectively pointing us towards information and knowledge which would be useful for personal and social life. It is in many people's profitable interest that most of us should remain semi-literate. But then, so are many of the persuaders themselves; and among them some of the more effective.

A slight diversion here, to justify withholding the title 'professional' from the majority of such people. To belong to a 'profession' means to have ethical principles towards your field of work and its practices. All professions, properly so called, have their own form of the Hippocratic oath, spoken or unspoken. Medicine is obviously a profession; so is teaching; and public service broadcasting; and the law; and a great range of other activities old and new for which severe training is necessary, and with that the absorbing of the principles of that work in relation to those outside to whom it is offered: all these change the occupation from a job of work to a profession.

Until recently, I would have thought 'pharmacy' a profession, since it is devoted to serving the public fairly in its need for pure medical products. Yet it was announced a few weeks before I began writing this paper that a new drug which seems to slow the progress of a disease of old age (such as Parkinson's) has now been released for public use, and that pharmacists are selling it for prices ranging from £60 to £200. That looks like inexcusable profiteering. Challenged, the spokesman (PR person) for the pharmacists responded in roughly this way: 'My members are professionals. They may charge what they choose' – which redefines, reduces and ethically denatures the meaning of the word 'professional'. This then means: 'We are free to make what profit we can: that's part of our definition of a 'profession'.

The great body of these relatively new styles of operator – men and women – are not professionals either, since they manipulate language and emotions so as to further the profits or increase the influence of those who employ them. It is a sad sign of their basic insecurity that they do cling to the word 'professional' to describe themselves; have Codes of Professional Ethics, Mission Statements, and the like. Since their ethics are never pure but always contingent – contingent on the need to deliver what those who pay them want (which is, itself, always and entirely contingent) – their self-designed tickets of entry to the professions can never be honoured at the entrance gates. They are parasitic on and compliant to activities which are never disinterested, always interested.

This takes us to the need for a literacy which is, obviously, not only beyond Level 4 – we have seen that that is elementary – but beyond also a degree of literacy which has absorbed information and knowledge adequate for the more complex practical managing of daily life. It points to the need, the inescapable need, for a degree or a kind of literacy which is alert to the manifold deceptions – carried mainly in language – by which persuasion operates in the open commercial society. The need is, above all, for Critical Literacy, literacy which is critically aware, not easily taken in, able to 'read' tricks of tone, selectivities, false *ad hominem* cries, and all the rest.

In the face of these assaults by television, radio, the Press, mail-shots and hoardings, the level of literacy required by Level 4 is depressingly inadequate – a vehicle without wheels. And 40 per cent do not pass at even that level. All that phoney language and distorted emotionalising so as to take money from the pockets of all those inadequately-educated people. A shameful travesty of a so-called democracy, a distortion of what Edward Shils rightly hailed as 'the entry of the working-class into society', of people most of whom now, happily, have money to spare after paying for necessities, but who are lured to misspend it by people most of whom are verbally cleverer than they are.

At this point some defenders, especially among the advertisers themselves, say: but most people are not taken in. Some are not, certainly, but many are. The figures prove this, as does the willingness of the advertisers to continue throwing money into their 'useless' efforts. Why are so many well-educated people, at all levels and in all sorts of occupations, ready to say not a word about this distorted application of the billions spent on education for, by now, more than a hundred years? It is just about a century since Britain was able to claim to be the first literate nation. Not to recognise this long failure, to brush it aside on behalf of others, is a form of unconscious populist contempt; 'stay as sweet as you are' as a justification for inaction.

Why do increasing numbers of head teachers agree to the use of child-directed advertising on their premises (soft drinks, crisps, chocolate)? Yes, we know many of them are hard up for school equipment, but that does not excuse an implicit abusing of their charges. This is Judas money, not to be excused by talk about 'living in the real world'; they should be ashamed to use such language.

Why do so many actors and actresses, among them predominantly the best paid in their profession, give their faces and voices to making claims they cannot substantiate about goods they don't themselves use? Where is the professionalism there?

From all this we have to adopt the slogan 'Literacy is Not Enough'. The level of literacy we accept for the bulk of the population, of literacy unrelated to the way language is misused in this kind of society, ensures that that literacy becomes simply a way of further subordinating great numbers of people. We make them just literate enough to be conned by the mass persuaders, for profit; truncatedly literate, two-dimensionally literate. One hears little of these considerations from the Department for Education and Employment.

The second slogan has, therefore, to be 'Critical Literacy for All'. Critical literacy means combining, with training in literacy, teaching about the difficulties, challenges and benefits of living in an open society which aims to be a true democracy. It means blowing the gaff on all the rampant small and large corruptions, on the humbugging, smart Alec persuaders; it means learning how to read the small print on insurance policies and guarantees on major purchases, telling the doorstep cowboys of all kinds to clear off, taking the mickey out of almost all television advertisements, especially those which go for our soft underbelly. It means using a fine, logical truth-toothcomb on all political manifestos ... and on a hundred other such things with which poorly-educated people are beset, even more than are the more effectively literate. Democracy is the least objectionable form of society, yes; but it has to be thought through and maintained in each generation. This is not being managed well today in any of the 'advanced' democracies. One encouraging thought is that there still exist remnants of the sceptical 'Come off it. Pull the other one ...' working-class tradition.

The simple conception of 'literacy' so much promoted today is inadequate. At its best it is like a bag of fairly simple plumbers' tools, where we need a set of fine surgical instruments. Profit-driven societies are marked by the disposition of the profit-seekers to push to the limits the rules their societies permit. They need a majority just literate enough to be hooked by every form of modern communication.

If people are made critically aware beyond that point then the profit-promoters will have to adjust, which they will do instantly, becoming ever so slightly less deceptive, less manipulators of linguistic sleight-of-voice, until one day, but not in our lifetime, they are indeed 'legal, decent, honest and truthful' in senses too subtle to be captured in the terms of reference of a government-appointed regulatory body. At that point they may even be entitled to apply for recognition as members of a profession.

From Critical Literacy to Creative Reading

Critical literacy is valuable – indeed, as I've said, essential, especially in a democracy – but still not enough. It is in its nature responsive to, reactive from, a state of affairs; and hence defensive. It says: 'If we wish this kind of society to release its potential, such and such steps will have to be taken, ranks will have to be drawn up against as many as possible of the parasitical and piratical forces which batten on to society's openness, which make it grow crooked, not straight.'

On the positive side, such a society must give all its members the opportunity to open their minds to the best kinds of creativity, to the best works of the intellect and imagination. Only through this can a 'society' begin to be a 'civilisation'. A society which does not recognise and honour this imperative will be populated by 'thriving earthworms', not cultivated humans. Of course, if people settle for being earthworms one cannot forbid them, but they should have the opportunity to see what they are missing.

Most well-educated people, asked to name the Queen of the Arts, will choose music, and I would not wish to demur. Nor would I wish to introduce pecking orders. I would only insist that literature is a very great art indeed and in some unique ways. It has a different language to that of music; indeed, to speak of 'the language of music' is to use a metaphor and one drawn from the main instrument of literature, words. Which seems like an irony, but isn't; it is, rather, a tribute to the importance of language as the root and rooted form of explicit communication.

The key lies in that word 'explicit'. Words are the most direct, avowed, available, demotic, everyday, form of communication. That is where other words employed above – 'root form' – come in; words are rooted in the everyday. I remember quite well my own introductions to the pleasure of words. The home was bookless, but an unmarried aunt living with her mother, as I a grandson was, had an unaware but acute sense of language. She picked up images like an amused jackdaw. I don't think she invented them; that would have been asking too much, but she knew good ones when she heard them. She would say of a woman with an aggressive stare: 'Ooh! Her eyes stuck out like chapel hat-pegs.' I remember Max Wall, the mad surrealistic music-hall comedian who broke away from the piano, transfixed his audience and asked us to consider what a beautiful word – its vowels drawn out – 'coalhole' is'; and the day I realised the beauty of 'drizzle', onomatopoeic, perfectly fitting the kind of English weather it describes: 'Oh, look! It's drizzling again.' No wonder some ad-man recently invented the title 'lemon zest drizzle cake'; almost enough to make you buy it. A French hotel brochure arrives and promises a breakfast buffet which is *copieux*; splendidly long vowels, the suggestion of wide-open generosity, a cornucopia.

Then there was Swinburne, read by chance in the Public Library at about 11 years old. Later I learned to scoff at his self-indulgences. I do not now; I remember the first lines which held me: 'When the hounds of spring are on winter's traces, / The mother of months in meadow or plain / Fills the shadows and windy places / With lisp of leaves and ripple of rain; ...'

Later, but still in adolescence, there was Melville and the *Maldive Shark*: 'About the Shark, phlegmatical one / Pale sot of the Maldive sea / The sleek little pilot-fish, azure and slim, / How alert in attendance be.' Movement recreated in sound, and an interplay of words both concrete and cultural. 'Phlegmatic ... sot ... alert ... in attendance ...' sway between the two suggestivities. An examiner demurred at one of my Final degree papers because I had quoted Wycherley on a woman who had: 'A jut with her bum that would stir an anchorite'. I thought it a brilliant, brief, erotic image. For me, as for people like me, that early affair with language was both physical – sensuous, on the pulses – and an introduction to possible exactness of thought, and response to imagination in action.

In literature, words can rise, be transmuted, leave the day-by-day so as to try to explore the most intricate and subtle elements of our lives – of relationships whether of love or hate, apprehension of the physical world, and intimations of a world outside; of all that makes up what we call our experience. It does all this through the love and developing understanding of words. That is why it can be called unique, irreplaceable.

We should, in this country, be exceptionally pleased that this is so, since literature is the one art in which we have excelled. Not in music, not in the visual arts – good though we may have been on some occasions at practising those – but in works of literature, in poetry, drama, the novel and all ancillaries. The French are properly proud of their own cultural achievements, but recognise that in literature we have been pre-eminent. It is a sad irony that that achievement is little recognised today, even by many people who would regard themselves as 'educated'. The terms by which we define education have changed. As an American writer said recently: 'Reading is what is left of us'; by which he meant that literature enshrines our experiences over the centuries, tries to order and interpret them and to do so, no matter how painful that may be, with honesty, in honest language. How much better can one confront life?

So little do so many people understand all this that growing numbers have come round simply to assuming that the immense development in modern communications technology will make reading obsolete, and that anyone who at all questions the unassailable onward march of that technology is a Luddite.

As was said earlier, modern communications technology has many and manifest rewards and it would be Luddite to regret it. But to think it will do away with reading is to misunderstand its nature and, even more, the nature of reading. These advantages, to pick up again a distinction made earlier, do make it easier to build on to fundamental literacy (as always the cornerstone) by assisting the acquisition of information and, if we choose to go to the trouble of using them in that way, of knowledge. So much is plainly to the good. What reading gives is something different; reading of value, it is here assumed, not the passive absorption of rubbish – of which there are increasing amounts nowadays.

Here we have to defend the use and meanings of several unfashionable words. To talk about the value of reading in itself is to talk of fine poetry, great dramas, good novels. It is to talk of works which show a respectful and gifted regard for language; a wish to sort out experience and, if possible, see some shape or meaning in it, and a desire to communicate those findings to those who will make the effort to read. A difficult apprenticeship but intensely worthwhile; a source of genuine not meretricious comfort and delight. These are times in which communal pleasures, things done within our peer groups or other collectives, seem self-evidently right. But to learn to read properly is to say: 'Stop the world. I want to get off'. For the time being; and intermittently. Reading is initially and inherently a solitary occupation. It leads through our eyes into our intellects and imaginations; and we absorb it in silence; although we can, afterwards, talk about it to whoever we will. Or we could listen to someone reading aloud to a group; but each member of that group has to try to absorb it as if alone. It is not and cannot in the first place be a group activity. In this it is very close to the absorption of music, even in large halls.

Reading is, therefore, a contract and an exchange between two people: the writer and the reader. The reader is not being given something without contributing something: his or her own responsiveness to language, to tone, to argument, to the stresses of the author's efforts to say what he really has to say. In return, the author's pleasure in that difficult success, if that is arrived at, is shared also. That is the basis of what I am calling Creative Reading. Its reward is that we are 'taken out of ourselves', 'rapt' into another world of the mind. We bring much to gain much. All this may come from honest literature. Dishonest literature, of which there is far more, is formulaic, routine in language and response, verbal marshmallow. It strokes our existing prejudices and laziness; it does not challenge.

What are called the classics or the canon are not selected by 'the elitists' just to show their superiority. They survive because some people in each generation find important enquiries into the business of being human in them, what we do right to call lasting or even universal qualities. They survive also because each generation can hear in them things which speak to their particular sense of themselves and their times. 'Universality' is all these things.

Such arguments are not popular today; they imply selection, a winnowing, that some books are poor and others better, that effort is needed in reading and some isolation. So we invent myths to make it all sound easy, even effortless. Such as: 'It doesn't matter what you read. At least you will have started, even if on trash. You can move on from there to better things.

Start on sex-and-violence junk and you will be likely to graduate to James Bond and so to Graham Greene and then to Conrad'. Have you ever met anybody who has made that splendid progress? Ill-founded hope trying to triumph over harsh reality.

We should not draw general conclusions from small minorities. Those of good native intelligence which includes a response to language will, in the beginning, read anything they can lay their hands on, from sauce bottles to advertisements in buses. They go on, on and up, through books specifically written for children to the surprisingly large number of books which one casually assumes are for adults but can entrance children also, especially if they are introduced to them through readings by their parents. Dickens is the model here.

Do most other 'readers' move on and up in that way? No, they go round and round, reading the same sort of thing. They provide a 'market' for repetitive reading of the same sort of thing; books which provide the same kind of plot, progress, denouement as all that went before, books which never disturb but repeat the same kind of easy effects. It is in the interests of those who produce such repetitive stuff to keep their customers hooked, coming back for more; that they do not go 'on and up' but 'round and round'. 'On and up' is myth number one, very comforting, very evasive and very mistaken.

Myth number two says that television adaptations are splendid gateways to reading. Look at the sales of *Pride and Prejudice* after the television version appeared, it is often said. Such adaptations are undoubtedly sources of pleasure. But they are in no way a substitute for the book, or a gateway to the reading of it. A great director taking off from a great book may make a great film, in its own right. It might then stand beside the book as a different form of art. It will not be a substitute for the book; and vice versa. Television adaptations (that is the key word) have to be selective of the original in quite radical ways. They have to stress what can best be carried over through the eye and angles of the camera, and often do that effectively; such as differences of pace as decided by the reader. But it is inherently a process which cuts out many aspects. Above all, and this is fundamental, a television version cannot carry tone of voice; and in most novels that is a – perhaps, the – critical bearer of meaning because it reinforces the implicit. To read a novel by Jane Austen is to engage with far more than fine costumes and fine scenes; or even with relationships, especially as carried in marvellously illustrative conversations. It is, first and foremost, to have all this transmitted to our inner ear by the voice of Jane Austen, that subtle range of ironic statement and implication which creates the Jane Austen 'experience' for us as we read it. But that is not part of television's communicative experiences. Which is why it is safe to assume, and we can find evidence in car boot sales and many other markets, that those 'books of the TV adaptation' are soon left unread after the first few paragraphs by all but those who already know how to read creatively, or are at the threshold of being able to do so. The television versions can be enjoyable, especially in the hands of a visually-gifted and inventive producer; they are not a substitute for silent reading.

What, though, about those who are not ready to go 'on and up' or to take off from watching a television adaptation? There is little point, though it sometimes helps, to be scornful of the popular reading of, say, 16-year-old girls. That is too easy and may well be off-putting. There can be a line, often thin but continuous, between novelettes and *Jane Eyre*; and some teachers have followed it successfully. That is one of the best challenges to teachers who care both for literature and for the education of adolescents. We need good writers, and good writers need good readers in every generation.

But for whom are writers writing these days? For their own kind, of course, for other writers; and for professional critics and reviewers; and for that wider circle who are often slightly contemptuously called 'the chattering classes', the 'intelligentsia' who read the broadsheets, listen to Radio 3, take journals of opinion. Yet, in a population of over 50 million, they are quite a small minority, in some respects an important minority, but not sufficient to provide the amount of intellectual yeast a pluralistic society needs.

Many thousands of graduates and professional people, many thousands of meritocrats, and many thousands of others without paper qualifications still compose the 'common readers', the 'intelligent laymen and women'. We cannot accurately count them, and those who say that 'unqualified' but intelligent lay readers are a dying breed may have a point. But not a totally convincing point. There is evidence enough from the sales of some books, the audiences for some radio and television programmes, the great numbers who go to classes in adult education, that there is still an audience out there much larger than that of the commonly received-and-labelled intellectuals.

This statement will not be accepted by many, least of all by many manifest intellectuals and academics themselves. 'When you say "We should …", who are the "we" whom you invoke and with such apparent confidence?' they ask. 'Have you not realised that your assumed old audiences, "the saving remnant", have all but disappeared?'

As I have said, the positive case is not provable. Almost through all its parts, this is an age of nervous relativism. Public voices fear they have lost credibility, especially when they start to compose sentences which begin 'We should ...'. Accredited intellectuals tend more and more to address only those in their own known circles; the broadsheets give more and more space to what seems the fashionable intellectual froth of the moment, less and less time and space to slower and more considered work. The comparison with the measured and confident tones of address to their assumed audiences which one finds in, say, late-Victorian authors is great.

Yet, though the old certainties about the existence of an identifiable group of 'serious' readers have been badly shaken, some who would like to write for them are still unwilling to give up hope. Probably those readers are less class-identifiable today and not embarrassed by that; nor should we be – quite the contrary; it is one sign of a more mature society, one in which a writer does not need to feel that certain tones of voice are needed for audiences from different social classes. More today will have had some form of higher education; many may have learned to be suspicious of the wooing voices aimed at the great bulk of the population. They may not all, though, have learned to suspect the more sophisticated persuasions aimed precisely at them – voices which aim themselves now at the broadsheets, the journals of opinion, and Channel 4. Still, though hardly any author today would be willing to announce that he 'rejoices to concur' with the views of his common readers, some authors can, after looking and listening all around, decide that such an audience does still exist and is as much as ever worth trying to reach.

The above lines may have given the impression that almost all writers have a hoped-for audience at the back of their minds. This is simply not so. Many writers, among them some of the very best, write 'because they have to' and in the practice of writing think little, if at all, of their likely audiences. They have an itch, an impulse, which will not be denied. Flaubert said writing is 'a dog's life, but the only one worth living'. Graham Greene saw writing as an escape from horrors even greater than those Flaubert suggested: 'Writing is a form of therapy; sometimes I wonder how all those who do not write, compose or paint can manage to escape the madness, the melancholia, the panic fear which is inherent in a human situation'. For writers such as these the reader may be hardly aware of being addressed. We are onlookers – 'on-listeners' – eavesdroppers. Of course they want their books to sell and be read. He who runs may read; they don't greatly want to know who is doing that; they prefer to get on with their dog's life, their form of therapy for madness, melancholia and panic.

Even in translation, Chekhov often sounds like a writer who combines both kinds of impulse. He is composed-whilst-composing, within himself; he neither woos nor frightens, but does not seem closed-off within himself; he extends a sort of grave courtesy towards those whom presumably, somewhere, somehow, he assumes will be reading him.

I said something much earlier and sketchily about what we may gain from reading books of quality. In making claims such as these, there is always a danger of afflatus, of appearing to present great literature as an all-embracing panacea. That impression needs to be qualified. It is remarkable how many fine writers have made great claims for their art, greater than most outsiders would dare to make, and greater than what one might have expected from them. Yet who is better to make such claims than those who have toiled in that quarry?

D. H. Lawrence said: 'You can't fool the novel – the one bright book of life'. Malraux was less uplifting, more warmly ironic when he remarked that the novel is one of the happier consequences of the fall of man.

Earlier authors, unsurprisingly, went wider and were grander. Carlyle did not spare the claims. From several of his writings there came: 'In books lies the soul of the whole past time ... A good book is the purest essence of the human soul ... If a book comes from the heart, it will contrive to reach other hearts ...' and 'All that mankind has done, thought, gained or been: ... is lying as in magic preservation in the pages of books. They are the chosen possession of man'.

Against that breadth of claim the contemporary critic who says: 'Culture does not (cannot) transcend the material forms and relations of production' sounds lame, hobbled by an ideologically-limiting strait-jacket of packaged explanation and response. It is the claim for 'inherent qualities' which worries such people, the assertion that some qualities, some books are more worthwhile and, therefore, require our serious attention more than others. We are back again with that nervous relativism: a relativism which, faced with a clearly distinguished and an equally clearly third-rate book, takes refuge in let-outs such as 'How can you make judgments between them? Surely each is *good of it's kind*?' No: one is 'good' by the severest standards of comparison; the other is not 'good' but may be 'effective' – effective for the populist job it sets out to do. The works of Jeffrey Archer, for example.

It follows that critics such as the one quoted above reject the idea of exemplary moments in literature (an aspect of Matthew Arnold's 'touchstones'). Such moments stick like burrs in the minds of others. Without effort one can recall them in Shakespeare, Wordsworth, Jane Austen, Dickens, George Eliot, Hardy, Lawrence; and in French, Italian, German and Russian works, even in translation. These are scenes – confrontations, revelations – which exhibit the power and beauty of language exploring – recreating, bodying out – the nature of our relationships, our responsibilities towards others, and (thank goodness) our inescapable duties towards the exercise of our own free-will, our fear and pity and joy – all drawn in 'material particularity ... the heft of things ... the solidity'.

Auden has some interesting and teasing passages on the superiority of the intuitive over the objective: 'In grasping the character of a society, as in judging the character of an individual, no documents, statistics, "objective" measurements can ever compete with the single intuitive glance'.

Such statements are plainly no more than assertions, unprovable. But people keep trying. In his book *The Western Canon*, Harold Bloom asserts yet again the autonomy of the imagination: 'Aesthetic criticism returns us to the autonomy of imaginative literature and the sovereignty of the solitary soul, the reader not as a person in society but as the deep self, our ultimate awareness'. Writers and readers are submerged in society, but the acts of creating and of reading literature detach both, provisionally, from the demands of society. They are contracts, compacts, between the work and the writer, the work and the reader, the writer and the reader. The solitary soul is within but greater than its social connectings; it is 'our ultimate awareness'.

All serious writing is about discrepancies, discordances and their possible resolution between the world outside as we would wish to see it and as we encounter it; between what others have made of it and what we are now making of it; between the world of relationships we inhabit and the world inside our selves. Gifted writers help us to see, to learn from and to enjoy the learning, better than we can manage ourselves.

Does all this, not only literature but the arts generally, help us to *be* better? Some people think so and more would like to think so. Doubters have much evidence on the other side; and usually start by invoking Hitler and his – very prescribed and predictable – love of music. Today, the doubters far outnumber the believers or would-be believers; such people are thought to belong to the late-nineteenth century when we could be assured of certain certainties; and are easily mocked: 'That line is the old humanist one about reading as a moral activity, the elemental legend that assimilating the contents of a printed page *automatically* makes you a better person ...'

The stressed 'automatically' is the weak plank in that piece of modish literary journalism. It would be difficult to find a thoughtful reader who thinks the process automatic. Emerson and Elizabeth Barrett Browning and many another provide the right counter-balances: 'There must be a man behind the book' and 'Books succeed / and lives fail'. Both of these can apply to both writer and reader.

If the first common myth about writing is that offshoot of relativism that there is a gifted writer inside each of us only awaiting release, then the second myth is the more old-fashioned, non-relativist, touching, earnest, hope that good writing has or certainly should have a link with good living, virtue, awakened or strengthened by books, in both writer and reader. Put so, that seems a plainly ingenuous assumption and would make the teaching of English literature even more important than it already is – the teacher as morality-injector. Yet the assumption has a rugged, limpet-like strength and staying-power. Surely someone who sees so far into the human psyche, who can recreate and, in certain ways, weigh acts and relationships of vice and virtue, of guilt and charity and tolerance, surely such a person will be affected for the better? 'We needs must love the highest when we see it'; much will then rub off on us? Surely to see all this, if only implicitly to judge it, and to be able to recreate it in memorable language, must indicate a talent, a character not detached from the morally-responsible person who possesses it – so we sometimes longingly ask?

I am given to this longing, residually. Seeing a man of about 35 years reading a paperback on the train, with his grimy boots placed on the seat opposite, I assumed that such a one would be reading a trashy novel, probably containing sex and violence. He closed the book and got up to go. *Great Expectations*. Surely those who read Dickens could be expected not to put their feet up on railway-carriage seats, I thought deflatedly.

Why can great writers be horrible people? Why not – is a fair counter-question? We can more easily keep the making and love of music in a separate compartment from that in which we act and justify our acts. It would be pleasant to think that by means of its own, unique 'language' music can civilise the soul in a way we would like to understand 'civilisation'; but there do not have to be such bridges. In writing, as in music, the gift falls on the just and the unjust. Auden often spoke of this: 'All will be judged. Master of nuance and scruple, / pray for me and for all writers, living or dead; / because there are many whose works / Are in better taste than their lives, ...'.

Literature, as we noted earlier, is, by its nature, of the earth, earthy. It explicitly uses words with earthy roots or moral weight for the things we think and do and the reasons why we so think and do. It rarely escapes from that condition; it is within itself aesthetic, but aesthetics is not the end of the matter. It is always ethically involved, caught up with the crime. That is why many assume, or perhaps only wish earnestly, that the two roles: our

handling of language to examine and recreate our worlds, and our responsibility for our own behaviour in this language-and-ethics-heavy world, are
inextricably bound.

Auden also liked to talk of three memorable writers who were deeply
flawed human beings: Yeats, Frost and Brecht. He thought them all self-
regarding. He was, of course, indicating that there is no necessary connection between being able, through moving language, to explore deep ethical
dilemmas and being able or willing to resolve them virtuously in ourselves.
It follows that what is sauce for the authorial goose should be sauce for the
reader gander; that we are not necessarily made better by reading 'great'
books, reading them thoroughly, being responsive to and understanding
their nuances, their penetrations, even their 'lessons'.

Yet Auden, and others, did not entirely deny any connection between our
reading and our moral sense. Surely, it might be said, there may be some
gain, but not an 'automatic' one, from having our minds exposed to such
relationships through the intervention of those whose minds and command
of language are subtler than ours? The acceptance of a more-or-less
inevitable link would reduce our free-will to decide our own way in life,
good or bad, even though we may have read, 'responded to', any number of
great writers. The best we may say, and it is a good and weighty best, is that
if we have been introduced to these works, have assessed them in our minds
and felt them on our imaginative pulses, and we go on sinning against that
light, we do so with our eyes open. We may then say that books of great
depth *stand available* to influence us, to nourish our spirit; if we so will.

Against all this, the current setting of communications technology against
the book, to the book's disadvantage, is revealed as muddled and shallow.
As here: 'One of the problems that calcifies the contemporary stand-off
between the average book-lover and the proponent of the bright technological future is the former's invariable descent into misty-eyed humanism ...
Regarding the book as a moral penicillin ... won't do now, and if we want
the book to hold its own against the VCR and the Information Superhigh-
way, one of the first things we should do is to treat it with a little less rever-
ence'. Camus is preferable: 'To write is to become disinterested. There is a
certain renunciation in art ...'. There is a cocky shallowness, a thinness of
intellectual texture, in talking about the book – Chaucer, Fielding, Smollett,
Dickens, Joyce, Lawrence, Mann, Proust, Leopardi, Cervantes, Borges,
and many others – as having to 'hold its own' against the VCR. What a
deprivation it would be not to have met, engaged with, some authors of the
quality of those listed above.

In case much of all that has gone so far sounds too demanding before it becomes enjoyable, we may remind ourselves that there are sensible rules of thumb along the way, most of them provided by authors, themselves. Francis Bacon recommended skipping some books, according to their interest and worth. Dr Johnson doubted whether one had to read all books from beginning to end, and reading any book only as inclination leads (not to follow fashion). E. M. Forster said that only those books which touch particular chords influence us. Cecil Day Lewis said there are favourable hours for reading any book as there are for writing one. Valéry said we read best those books for which we are personally ready.

Finally, from a great many, a few more testimonies from those who have trodden the path, tried to look at their lives straight and whole – not self-justificatorily only. Nietzsche: 'We have art that we may not perish from the truth'. Kafka: 'A book must be the ice-axe to break the frozen sea within us'. Emerson: '[a book] builds a road into chaos and old night'. Samuel Butler: 'Yet meet we shall, and part, and meet again / Where dead men meet on lips of living men'.

Much more remains in books than the Captains and Kings have left behind or will leave. They reduce Hitler and Stalin and all their predecessors to the status of examples. And will continue to do so no matter how advanced our communications technologies may become; they are, again in Auden's words, 'rooted in imaginative awe'.

Part Two   Reading contexts

People say that life is the thing, but I prefer reading.
Logan Pearsall Smith

There are worse crimes than burning books.
One of them is not reading them.
Joseph Brodsky

An irrelevant education
Michael Schmidt

The *Bookseller* of 8 March 1996 carried statistics of 'Books Recorded for 1995': a total of 95,064 new titles and 'revised and new editions' published in the UK between January and December, an increase of 6,346 over 1994 (7.1 per cent). The 1996 'Books Recorded' broke into six figures. In 1995, fiction fell slightly, but every other major category grew. One thousand, nine hundred and forty-four poetry titles were recorded, of which just over 10 per cent were revised and new editions, 115 translations, and 16 limited editions. Prices remained stable, at just below the rate of inflation. It's no surprise that a (now retired) publisher recently suggested at an Arts Council seminar that subsidies should be given to publishers *not* to publish – like EC subsidies not to sow certain crops.

The news isn't quite so spectacular as it may seem. Statistics are compiled from registered ISBNs (International Standard Book Numbers); a pamphlet or vanity press book just as a huge *Collected Poems* is published with an ISBN. English-language titles from abroad often bear a British ISBN if distributed here by a major agency.

And books of poetry include new poetry, texts and anthologies produced for the academic market. In the listing for 'Publications of the week' in the same issue of the *Bookseller*, there are 15 poetry books including a Chaucer, an edition of Michelangelo's poems, Pope's *Homer* (a new Penguin Classic for a stout Cortez), and pamphlets. No bookshop could have stocked a full range of significant 1995 poetry, classics and translations and also carry a backlist. The task of sorting grain from chaff is more difficult than ever for bookseller and buyer. And despite the abundance of product, what you look for is seldom to be found.

As an undergraduate at Oxford, I was walking on Boars Hill with a friend. He began reciting some lines of Chatterton. It was, he said, part of the Minstrel's song from the medievalising play *Aella*:

> Comme, wythe acorne-coppe and thorne,
> Drayne mie hartys blodde awaie;
> Lyfe and all yttes goode I scorne,
> Daunce bie nete, or feaste by daie.
> My love ys dedde,
> Gon to hys death-bedde,
> Al under a wyllowe tree.

I knew of Chatterton from Wordsworth's *Resolution and Independence*, which carried the poet's name further in time and space than any other tribute: 'I thought of Chatterton, the marvellous Boy, / The sleepless Soul that perished in his pride.' Coleridge was behindhand. For over 30 years he tinkered with his *Monody on the Death of Chatterton*, spoken figuratively at the poet's grave (a pauper suicide, his grave was unmarked). Coleridge's significant poetic debt to Chatterton is in the metrical organisation of *Christabel*.

When I went to Blackwell's I discovered that there was no edition of Chatterton in print. This was even before the terrible famine of authoritative texts set in in earnest. A year later I could find no edition of Swift's poems, of the plays and verse of George Peele, or the poetry of Crashaw, or Cowley, or Barnes. Indeed, if I recall, at the time it was even hard to lay one's hands on the poems of Christina (and how much more difficult Dante Gabriel) Rossetti.

In the 1970s and 1980s, biography proliferated. There were lives of Ford Madox Ford and Wyndham Lewis, the Powyses and many others, even though their works were generally unavailable. The higher gossip, as it came to be called, displaced the work itself. Or rather, the work itself had already been displaced, and what survived was not the *monuentum aere perennius* but the *vita. Ars brevis, vita longa* as it were. Biographers received advances larger, in some cases, than the entire literary earnings of their subjects. This was the triumph of narrative, or of prurience, the intentionalist fallacy carried into the heart of *oeuvre* after *oeuvre* with a sense that a biographer could *understand* the warmth and content in the cold facts of a life.

What was occurring – and the occurrence has accelerated in the last 10 years – was the privileging of the present and of present perspectives over the past and, within the present (since contemporary literature has become part of the school and university curriculum), the establishment of an educational (and commercial) canon. In poetry, a very few writers were singled out and published in school editions. Their work, for teachers and young readers, *was* modern poetry. By a perverse metonymy the part displaced the whole. Over the years the foregrounded poets change from time to time, but the selection has been, in formal terms, predictable: poets for whom there is a ready-made language of criticism, or a political rationale, at secondary and tertiary level.

Schools and universities are a market, and in any market it behoves the producer to manufacture market leaders. A poet who makes it on to the secondary school syllabus can sell 10,000 or 12,000 books a year and give numerous readings at fees of between £150 and £1,000 a throw. A poet who doesn't will be lucky to sell, after the first year, more than 100.

The privileging of the present means that it is possible to get through A levels with only the sketchiest knowledge of writing before the twentieth century – even of writing from before the Second World War. The works generally chosen are those which can be talked about: thus recent developments include the addition to the curriculum of verse which is topical in terms of the social politics of the age, a kind of tokenism on the one hand and of civicism on the other; cultural studies are well and truly in place. In a multicultural society the only intolerances permitted are those directed at the older culture: Milton was fair game to Eliot because of what Eliot deplored in his literary legacy; Spenser, Sidney, Shakespeare, Ralegh and others are fair game today because of their assumed political and social attitudes, their colour and gender, the conventions within which they worked.

The avant-garde poet, critic and translator Christopher Middleton most eloquently celebrated the importance of irrelevance in education. A distinguished educator, he deplored the insistence in the American curriculum on recommending texts to which students could 'relate'; he kicked against the tendency to praise ancient writers by calling them 'modern' and 'contemporary'. The *other* is what leads us away from where we are, leads us forward even when that *other* is in the past. This is what Eliot and the great Modernists knew. Accessing the past did not mean reading poor translations of Virgil and imagining one had got hold of the *Aeneid*. It meant learning languages and histories. Within English it meant understanding linguistic and semantic change, coming to grips with earlier contexts: the religious and political struggles of the seventeenth century, as registered in the writing of the age, told Eliot more about the nature of English culture and the nature of cultural loss even than the two world wars he lived through did. When, a couple of years ago, Eliot's successors at Faber published an anthology of versions of Ovid 'translated' by various hands, among the poets contributing only a handful knew Latin well enough to work from the originals. For the rest the 'tales' were a pretext. C. H. Sisson speaks of translation as 'fishing in other men's waters' – he should know, as one of the best translators of our time. But the majority of the poets in the Ovid anthology were fishing in their own waters with another man's bait.

Was it Ernst Gombrich who sent his students to study the Raphael Cartoons at the Victoria and Albert Museum and, when one of them did not deliver her essay because she 'didn't like them', declared, 'I didn't ask you to write about yourself, I asked you to write about Raphael.' Few teachers nowadays have the force of character or the educational remit to direct their students so forcefully. In creative writing groups candidates often seem to demand mercy and charity rather than critical candour.

The only way a writer or reader can get a purchase on language and on imaginative literature is through wide and (ideally) disciplined reading. Without a sense of continuities, multiculturalism itself becomes an empty term. Spenser was expendable. Milton is expendable. Some argue that Shakespeare, too, can be disregarded. Initially, the move against the English classics was seen as a radical mode of cultural enfranchisement: such poetry was 'difficult' in formal and semantic terms; it excluded some readers who could not or would not make the effort, or who – given their own cultural antecedents – found it pointless. Let all readers, therefore, be emancipated from its rigours.

The result is impoverishment, to the extent that in teaching first-year undergraduates Renaissance poetry one discovers that they have no sense of what the Renaissance was (in England or elsewhere); have not heard of Herbert and Marvell and Chapman. In teaching 'modes' – the pastoral for example – one discovers that at most one in a dozen has read Gray's *Elegy*. Few are familiar with the King James Bible and the Book of Common Prayer (the syllabus is rigorously secular). But traditional hymns and carols are still relatively familiar and make a useful, perhaps a single, point of common departure in the discussion of form and formal language.

Walking on Boars Hill in the 1960s, I was 19 and not unique among my contem- poraries in being besotted with poetry. I asked my friend who had recited Chatterton to prepare a selection of his poems. I asked other friends to make selections of Christopher Smart, George Peele and Richard Crashaw. And I published these authors because I wanted their work to be available to people who, like me, wanted to fill in the gaps around the great poets with the good poets, many of whom are certainly not 'minor' except in comparison with the veritable giants. Over the years the list, which we called Fyfield Books after Arnold's Fyfield Elm, has included the work of 60 or more writers from the fourteenth to the twentieth century whose absence from the bookshelves seemed to me and my friends an injustice, not only to the neglected writer but to the modern reader and to our literature.

Such acts of recovery and reappraisal are today generally conducted in the name of a movement or cause. Thus Virago and The Women's Press recovered numerous neglected women writers – though they omitted to recover quite a few who were not ideologically sound, or who were difficult and unlikely to sell well. Such enterprises are of value. Because no special interest attaches to Skelton, Chapman, Drayton, Surrey or Gascoigne, they will be read only in a culture that values *itself* in all its historical complexity and understands that, while Milton is not a modern, he is a measure of the Mod-

ern. Without him the pleasures we take in present culture will be ephemeral: we will celebrate the politically alert and inventive but semantically and formally impoverished work of Benjamin Zephaniah, the polemical fatuities of Adrian Mitchell, the sentimentalisms of Jenny Joseph, against a blank backdrop.

What counts now, according to booksellers with whom the *Bookseller* discussed buying, are three factors: imprint, design, and the media exposure a poet receives. Established imprints have an advantage: Faber, Penguin and Oxford are welcome, while all but a few smaller imprints find entry hard. The invisibility of significant avant gardes has to do with market – not readership – discipline: how the product looks, how and by whom it's marketed. In such a market-place the past and the foreign are strenuously neglected.

Most disheartening is that consolidation of a culture of 'market leaders': approved authors, who command feature coverage or syllabus exposure, whose presence is journalistically verified, who perform well in public – a tiny portion of authors of the 1,944 poetry books of 1995. 'In a market reeling from the effects of escalating costs and thinner margins following the ending of the Net Book Agreement, the *Bookseller* for 22 March 1996 declared, '[publishers] need to tailor products to ever-changing buyer profiles'. That discipline affects poetry, including 'rediscoveries' of authors whose presence might be a generative resource.

This situation, to a lesser degree, has existed for a long time. Christopher Ricks in *Essays in Appreciation* quotes Hallam Tennyson's *Memoir* about the attraction of biography: 'What business has the public to want to know all about Byron's wildnesses? He has given them fine work, and they ought to be satisfied. It is all for the sake of babble'. Even *Don Juan* is lost to the life, or those aspects of the life which make for spicy babble: Byron's *Greek Love*, that sort of thing.

There is another market force: poetry that 'succeeds' in Britain at present is 'accessible', makes limited demands. *Poetry Review*, 'the UK's most popular poetry magazine, is relaunching this spring with a stylish new look', a press release headed '*Poetry Review* Updates Its Image' informed us. It also came clean about its orientation. The editor opened the new-look magazine 'with a hard-hitting theme "How the Century Lost its Poetry"'. With characteristic syntactical symmetries he tells us: 'The fragmentation of metre urged by Pound and the dislocation of imagery enjoined by Eliot were mutually reinforcing. Together they were a very effective pantomime horse indeed'. It is hard not to conclude that the locus of the century's loss is in such critical facility. If we are safe now from the menace of Modernism, we are probably safe from poetry *tout court*.

Neil Belton, editorial director of Granta Books, wrote in *Index* (Issue 2, 1996) about the wider publishing environment in which attitudes such as *Poetry Review*'s thrive: 'What is disturbing in the great publishing combines is the emergence of a defiant populism among the executives who run them, for whom "literary" is a dirty word ... The polemic against "elitism" that accompanies this determination is strange; it is like watching city gents in pin-stripe suits stripping to their Y-fronts and dressing up in paint and feathers. It's a deliberate barbarism, like Murdoch's: you can market tits and serial killers, which proves that that is what people want ... Publishing should be driven by the desire to "make it strange", in a good old modernist phrase'. Serious American, Irish, Indian – *foreign* – English-language readers looking at the poetry that's made headway in Britain in recent years might be forgiven for finding the fare a bit thin, the wrong kind of democracy at work, in which a coarsened public opinion mis-values the bracing pleasure of R. S.Thomas's poems, or John Peck's. An environment such as this can undermine the genuine talents of writers like Carol Ann Duffy and Tony Harrison. What is the fuss about, the foreign reader asks – and finds the heart of British poetry somewhere else: not in Spender but in Bunting and MacLean, not in Harrison but in Hill, not in Armitage but in Constantine. If there are prizes for poets, they are less the bursaries, public awards and feature articles than the non-negotiable rewards of a demanding readership. In *Index* (Issue 2, 1996) Nadine Gordimer quotes Walter Benjamin's lucid proposition: 'One of the foremost tasks of art has always been the creation of a demand which could be fully satisfied only later'.

Downhill all the way? The commercialisation of publishing
Rivers Scott

It was Edward Heath who coined the phrase 'the unacceptable face of capitalism' – possibly his greatest achievement. When he did so he had his own targets in mind and, so far as I know, they did not include the book business. They might have done, all the same. Is it acceptable, for instance, as has happened more than once over the past two decades, for the owners and managers of once illustrious, independent publishing firms (often self-proclaimed left-wingers) to run those firms into the ground, sell out to a large conglomerate, walk off with more than a million pounds each, and leave their former employees to fend for themselves? Surely not. But those are one-off disgraces. What readers, writers and the staff of publishing houses really have to worry about are matters connected not only with money, but also with the whole of our rapidly changing cultural scene and the technology that goes with it.

Let us indulge in a bit of nostalgia. In the extensive and once familiar folklore of the book trade there is a story (not apocryphal, I believe) about Mr Gladstone and his printer, with whom the G.O.M., notwithstanding his enormous workload, liked to correspond while his books were going through the press. On the occasion in question Gladstone received his set of galleys, marked them up, sent them back, but found, at the next stage, one change still unmade. He wrote back to the printer saying 'Would you please make the correction'. The printer replied that he would certainly make the *change*, if Mr Gladstone absolutely insisted, but he could not make the correction since what the Prime Minister had now inserted was not correct.

Those were the days – and, of course, they are long gone. Most printers, even then, did not 'read' what they were printing (on the whole, the safest policy). Now we have computers which unfortunately can't read either: they can spell but not think – cannot tell you What is Watt. So it is back to the human factor and the first of the problems besetting editors and others in publishing houses today.

When I joined Hodder & Stoughton from Fleet Street some 22 years ago, one of the first things that struck me, apart from the friendliness of my colleagues and the then heads of the firm, was the meticulous, painstaking and loving way in which every single book was produced. I had a delightful, small office, hexagonal in shape, from the window of which, if I craned out a little way, I could see the dome of the British Museum Reading Room. I had a secretary and an assistant. Above all, from the point of view of service to my own and my fellow-editors' authors, there were two young women in a large room on the top floor whose sole allotted task was to copy-edit the typescripts. They checked spellings; they checked facts; and, as if the work they put in was not enough, some of the most important non-fiction titles were sent out to one particular indexer who was, in his main employment, a reader on the staff of a top daily London newspaper and who not only compiled an invariably masterly index but also looked out for any remaining discrepancies and errors.

That time has gone too. Such luxuries are now considered totally uneconomic. And if I was still in the position I held then I would no longer have a secretary but would, with the aid of my hard-pressed assistant, be shovelling through probably some 30 or more books a year to which I could not possibly give my full attention. Editors I know have resigned because of this. One of the best was not long ago thrown out because, as a director of the company frankly explained to me, 'there's no room for such people any more'.

This cannot but be a loss. There can, it is true, be such a thing as over-editing. In the United States particularly, where the great Maxwell Perkins, editor and mentor of Scott Fitzgerald and Ernest Hemingway, can be a dangerous guide to the less gifted, there are editors who dislike, or fail to understand, the style of many British authors and will take it upon themselves, if allowed to get away with it, to transform these writers' idiosyncrasies into a painful pedestrian plod. But the craft of true editing, which is what is now at risk, was a boon to all concerned: first to the writer, who welcomed the support and guidance, and then to the reader, who, unknowingly, reaped the benefits.

There are still some canny editors who manage to get round this problem. It depends in part what sort of works they are handling. Gimmicky books, for instance, need skill in presentation more than care over the prose. What is ominous is the number of worthwhile books that are being excluded from publication altogether. This 'death of the mid-list', as it is coming to be called, is also, obviously, the result of financial pressures. In the case of the large, publicly-quoted conglomerates in particular (and they are getting larger and larger), it is not just a question of 'Will this book make us money', but 'Will this book make us enough money? Will it be worth all the time and outlay expended on it?' This is tragic for some authors and of course, once again, a loss to the reader. And it is a fairly recent phenomenon. When my partner and I started up our literary agency at the end of 1981, we reckoned that if a book was good enough and we believed in it, however minority its interest, we would eventually find a home for it. We cannot say that any more, and I think most other agents would agree with us.

It is also a fact that ageism, however disguised or even unconscious, has made its presence disagreeably felt. Most of the wildly inflated advances for fiction, which get newspaper publicity and cause so much envy and grief to the 99.9 per cent of good authors who just go on writing, are paid to young novelists who have never been heard of before and in many cases will never be heard of again. It has been suggested (rightly, I suspect) that what the publishers who pay these sums are in fact doing is taking a huge and desperate gamble. They hope each time that the book they are signing up will make them a lot of lolly and save their financial skins. Whatever the reason, many struggling, would-be authors – and some even formerly-established authors still with loyal though no doubt diminishing readerships – are now not even finding agents. What would be the point in an agent taking on an author he knows he can't sell?

There are, unfortunately, further factors to compound this picture of gloom. One is the importance nowadays given to the views of the sales force. This is in no way intended as a disparagement of the sales staff themselves. They are the salt of the earth, beloved, respected and treasured within their firms, and in my day to be invited to join the men (it was an all-male cast then) in one of their bedroom soirées where, armed with a couple of bottles of whisky and an assortment of tooth mugs, they sat around slagging off the senior management and grumbling like old soldiers, was the greatest compliment any newly-joined editor could be paid. But the point about salesmen is that they know what has sold, not what will sell. At Hodder in the old days, no salesman (not even the sales director) was allowed near the weekly editorial conference. The editors chose the books and the salesmen were told to sell them. And that was the end of the matter.

If this seems rather a technical consideration, the next one is not. It is the dismayingly limited historical and literary reference span displayed by many young editors today. There is a story told about the late Harold Ross, the great editor of *The New Yorker*, a fanatical scrutineer of every page of his magazine, but a man whose knowledge contained some surprising gaps. In a short story he was checking there appeared a passing reference to the woman taken in adultery (John, 8: 2–11). 'Who she?', Ross scribbled in the margin of the proof. 'Has not appeared in the story before'. That used to be taken as a terrific joke, at the expense of a true, but eccentric, near-genius. Now it risks appearing quite commonplace.

What has to be remembered is the enormous extent to which both the cultural and the economic climate in Britain have changed in a very few years. Far more people now get their daily news from TV and radio than from reading of any sort. The young read less than the old, and no doubt this fact, as well as local authority cuts, has contributed to the steep and continuing decline in the sales of books to libraries; a catastrophe in every way.

Against this should be set at least one cheering factor – the presence of the band of small, thrusting publishers, and some not so small ones, now in existence and still starting up, with the ability to back their hunches in the old, traditional way. This is the acceptable face of capitalism, of which the book trade stands so much in need. May such firms continue to multiply and thrive.

Revolution in the book trade
Christopher Sinclair-Stevenson

I became a publisher in January 1961, joining the small but distinguished firm of Hamish Hamilton more or less straight from Cambridge. I left publishing to become a literary agent in February 1995. During those 34 years I witnessed a series of upheavals and fundamental changes in publishing which were startling mainly for their frequency, and for their ferocity.

Publishing by the early 1960s had not essentially altered since the inter-war years. Most companies were family-owned and family-run, or, at the very least, controlled by a number of editorial publishers (the emphasis being on the word 'editorial'): Faber and Faber, Chatto and Windus, Jonathan Cape, Longman's, Hart-Davis, Macmillan, the Bodley Head, Constable, Secker and Warburg, John Murray – and Hamish Hamilton. There were, of course, internal structural differences, but Hamish Hamilton was reasonably representative of the accepted norm. It had been started in 1931 by the eponymous Hamish Hamilton, and was run by him and his editorial partner, Roger Machell. There was a finance director and a production director. There was a children's books department and an educational books department. There was a sales manager (note: not director). Rights were handled by Roger Machell. There was no publicity department; marketing would not have been understood as a concept.

The annual output was about 70 titles in all. Hamish Hamilton (premises in Great Russell Street, on the fringes of Bloomsbury) had its own warehouse, a short stroll away in Covent Garden. It even had a trade counter where the main London booksellers could pick up copies of bestsellers.

It all sounds positively Arcadian. There were, inevitably, a number of worms in the bud, not all of them invisible. London publishing was an hermetically closed shop. If you were in, very good; if you were out, or even on the fringes, rather less good. It was difficult for that remarkable group of entrepreneurial publishers, who had come from eastern Europe before and shortly after the Second World War, to be accepted in an environment which often seemed to be based in the bar of the Garrick Club rather than in publishing offices. George Weidenfeld needed his Nigel Nicolson, and André Deutsch his Diana Athill and Nicolas Bentley.

Books and authors were often taken on because of friendship or recommendation. The power of the agent was comparatively weak, though some deference was reluctantly paid to Curtis Brown, A. P. Watt, A. M. Heath and David Higham. Once a writer had been taken on, he or she was expected to stay. The subsequent mobility of authors was not even considered as a nightmare possibility. There were stables of authors (the horse-racing metaphor was apt, as very often whole families were duly published under the same imprint). The publishers and the writers and the literary editors of the most influential newspapers and magazines all appeared to know one another. The right book seemed invariably to be placed in the hands of the right reviewer, who uncannily often produced the right notice. That was how reputations were formed, and it was a chain which seldom allowed an extra link of a, perhaps, baser metal.

When did it all change? In the late 1960s, winds of change were not confined to the African continent. Words like 'synergy' and phrases like 'multi-media conglomerates' were spoken, though rarely understood. Businessmen like Roy Thomson began to flex their muscles. He owned newspapers and television companies: surely the acquisition of book publishing companies could only enhance his ambition to control a substantial part of the written and spoken-word sector.

Among a number of companies he bought Hamish Hamilton and, slowly, there began a shift of power which accelerated when the Thomson Group was in due course sold to Penguin. Editors, notoriously, did not understand figures (the amounts of money involved were seldom great, so it did not appear to matter). So, their importance diminished, and the rule of the accountants began. There were, inevitably, some advantages and some ominous signs. A greater emphasis was placed on budgets and profit-and-loss accounts, as well as on sales, marketing and publicity. Boardrooms now represented every aspect of a publishing operation. Much of this was highly beneficial to both publishers and authors.

But there were equally considerable drawbacks. There was a new concentration of volume so that more and more books appeared; if only to fuel the printing works which some publishers also owned, and the expensive warehouses and distribution services which nearly all publishers owned. A list consisting of a mere 70 titles a year was not thought viable. Now, there were glossy catalogues with 70 titles every season.

The hoped-for synergy did not materialise. The cosy agreements between publishers and the people in the newspaper offices who bought the serial rights and devised the book pages may have been deplorably exclusive, but they worked. In an industry which was developing and expanding in such an uncontrolled and, indeed, uncontrollable way, personal contacts, particularly between editors and authors, were thought to be less essential than meetings.

The realisation dawned in many a corporate boardroom that there was no real profit in publishing unless a radically new approach was formulated.

And so a further shift of emphasis was introduced. Editors were tolerated because they were still the link with the writers, but their eccentricities and extravagances were frowned upon in this bright and brisk new world. Marketing was king. It was the marketing departments who really knew what would sell and, therefore, what should be bought. Paradoxically, publishing houses now paid out even greater sums of money, sometimes for the small number of high-profile, bankable authors who might be lured from one house to another; sometimes for new, young, photogenic writers with absolutely no track record (this was considered to be a positive advantage). Marketing directors rightly perceived this development as a kind of licence for self-perpetuation. The more money that was spent on acquiring a book, the more money had to be spent, additionally, on promoting that book. And glittering rubbish was often easier to market than a high-class novel or biography.

It *was* a self-fulfilling prophecy, but of a rather different nature. As the importance, or power, of the editor declined, so, too, did the editorial care and attention given to manuscripts either in progress or when they were delivered. Editors' time and concentration had been diverted elsewhere. Standards fell, partly because editors moved from house to house with often dazzling speed, thus depriving writers of that essential security and continuity; and partly because it was thought to be more cost-effective to use freelance editors, who often never even met the writers they were supposed to be editing.

There had been other shifts in the book world as a whole. In the early 1960s, virtually every order made by a bookshop to a publisher's representative was a firm sale. Few books were returned because they did not sell. In subsequent decades, as the power of the bookshop groups rose, and the days of the old-style stock-holding bookshop (in other words, a shop which would maintain a permanent selection of the titles that any self-respecting bookseller felt obliged to have always available) were seen to be numbered, the threat of ever-increasing returns was only matched by ever-increasing discounts granted by publishers to booksellers in a vain hope of securing their support. And, as the number of titles published increased year after year, so, too, did the rate of returns grow.

The second major factor was the change in the library sector. The strength of the public library system in Britain had always been the envy of other countries. In the 1960s and even later, it was held that it was impossible to sell less than 2,000 copies of almost any book, unless it was of an amazingly rarefied nature. Suddenly, central government funding and support from local authorities fell dramatically. The best-selling authors flourished, if anything, even more. But first-time writers fared considerably less well.

The third factor was the increase in importance or, at least, relevance, of the agent. Many authors felt that the upheavals in publishing, with companies being bought and sold and bought and sold again, with imprints vanishing, and with editors becoming an endangered species, worked against their interests. Agents, by the nature of their business, were more stable and could offer more long-term advice and support. The impact of television, though often cited, was exaggerated.

In the space of nearly four decades I have witnessed a revolution in the book trade. Many, indeed the great majority, of the old independent companies have been swallowed up; sometimes spat out; always changed. There are a few survivors: John Murray, Faber and Constable; and Bloomsbury, Orion and Harvill from more recent establishments. Bookshops, equally, are divided between the groups and the decreasing number of independents. Agents have become more influential.

So much for the market in general, and for the structure of the publishing industry in particular. What about the quality of publishing? It is certainly far more difficult for an editor, unless he or she is remarkably resilient or has an unassailable reputation, to build a list of authors who can be allowed to develop over a number of books. Indeed, this is one of the most recognisable changes in publishing over the last 40 years. A gradual build-up in popularity is too slow. The quaint concept of an author remaining for many years with the same publisher is considered wholly unrealistic.

A curious example of a situation where an editor prefers to show loyalty to his author and, indeed, vice versa, rather than to his employer occurred in early 1998. HarperCollins, owned by Ruper Murdoch's conglomerate News International, had commissioned the former Governor of Hong Kong, Chris Patten, to write a book about the Far East. His editor stated publicly that it was an exceptionally good book; Rupert Murdoch was alarmed at some of Patten's less than complimentary remarks about the Chinese, and demanded that the contract for the book should be cancelled. The editor departed; the book moved to another publisher. There was considerable breast-beating in the book world, and considerable embarrassment within HarperCollins and News International. The incident, unimportant in the long run, did demonstrate two facts of life: the author/editor relationship is still strong, and owners of conglomerates have power.

Technology has provided the other most salient change. Desktop publishing, computers and word processors, fax machines and e-mail; all of these would have been considered Wellsian flights of fancy in 1961.

So, the technology, the infrastructure and the power base have all altered. The people, by and large, have not. Authors still want to write books and still feel, or at least hope, that there is an appreciative audience out there somewhere. Editors, if they are allowed to, want to edit, encourage, above all to feel part of the whole process of publishing. Fashions in books have inevitably shifted. Travel, popular science, gardening and cookery, move up and down the sale scale. Even the size of a book has gone through a number of permutations: from small, to enormous, back to small. But the word continues.

The flexible bookshop
Enid and Chris Stephenson

One of the most important outcomes of the National Year of Reading will be what happens once the 'year' is over. For this reason, the observations below are offered as suggestions for some possible ways ahead. They are gleaned from 18 years' experience of independent bookselling, during which, with deliberate intent, 'bookselling' came to mean not just the usual over-the-counter commerce between buyer and seller, but very often a dedicated involvement in and instigation of extra-curricular activities: book events – of all shapes, sizes, hues and complexions, in which adults' and especially children's books were promoted, shared, celebrated. It was a wholehearted attempt to broaden the scope and boundaries of the traditional bookshop, whenever necessary moving out into the larger community to wherever the particular event was taking place; at times, almost a rejection of the usual concept of a 'bookshop', a specific area in a fixed location. Hence the *flexible* bookshop.

The fact that this essay is written from a standpoint of *book*selling gives immediate endorsement to the view that literacy – implying the barest minimum skills for comfortable survival in a print-based society (though that in itself is no mean achievement!) – cannot be regarded as an end in itself. Even the ability to read a newspaper, though doing so can certainly help keep the critical faculties in trim, has about it the distinct air of merely functional literacy. 'Newspapers,' wrote Charles Lamb, 'often excite curiosity. No one ever lays one down without a feeling of disappointment.' No, what concerns us here is that one step beyond the purely functional, into a literacy that centres on the reading of books which engage, entertain, unbend the mind, free the imagination and which can 'think for me' (Lamb again). And while the 'ordinary reader' rarely heads out for the higher reaches of Literary Criticism (which often gives the impression, it seems, of being an end in itself), there can be little doubt that the more prolific and searching that reader becomes the more the inner critical and creative process is awakened. This 'searching' need be no more than friendly discussion, for there is nothing so stimulating as an exchange of views with like-minded fellow-readers (which includes, or should include, bookshop assistants). Ideally then, bookshops and the general areas of libraries should be abuzz with excited chat; alive with the exchange of ideas, suggestions and opinions. (There is nothing more toe-curling than the parent who whispers to the child 'Remember, keep quiet – and don't touch the books!')

In any discussion about literacy, the fundamental importance of children's books should never be underestimated, for in the majority of cases it is in childhood that literacy begins. The wealth and quality of British children's books are unsurpassed, making the shabby way in which they are treated by the media (i.e. largely ignored) shameful to the point of being criminal. In endeavouring to redress the balance it is imperative that specialist children's bookshops, libraries and the vitally important Federation of Children's Book Groups (branches of which can be found in many, but as yet not enough, areas of the country) provide a continuously sustaining platform of advice, information, knowledge, encouragement and support, punctuated by imaginative (not just publishers' publicity balloons and Peter Rabbit costumes!) book events. Furthermore, they must go out into the community and meet the potential readers or customers, never just sit back and wait. Be flexible.

When it was allowed to function, Writers in Schools, consisting for the most part of a one-off prearranged visit by a writer to a particular school and administered by regional Arts Councils, could be a simple and effective scheme. Unfortunately, much of its vibrancy has now been eviscerated by a new insistence on 'structured visits', which come as a complete 'package' with components including the inevitable workshops, follow-up visits and – manna to the administrative mind – final reports. What should be a unique occasion, allowing a change of perspective from the normal day-to-day teaching and learning process, has been strait-jacketed and subsumed by the structured curriculum. There can be little doubt that the best Writers in Schools visits occurred when a mild, but detectable, whiff of – dare one say it? – the anarchic (as in 'non-recognition of authority') wafted from them.

Three brief examples of this 'anarchistic' approach in action: first, Shirley Hughes talking and showing her artwork to an enthralled First School audience – except for one small girl who, in spite of a number of admonishments from others, insisted on spending the entire talk with her back firmly turned towards the speaker. Shirley Hughes remained unperturbed by this display of seeming indifference, an attitude entirely vindicated at the conclusion when it became apparent that the girl had not only listened to every word of the talk, but by whatever means had also managed to see every piece of artwork perfectly clearly. Then, Hugh Lupton, the storyteller, performing to a group of Middle School students. The tough all-lads-together-at-the-back were determined to register their lack of co-operation with smirks and noisy shufflings of their hi-tech trainers. Hugh fixed his eyes on them: 'Right. Listen to this ...' He began to tell a ghost story. Everyone, all ears – even and especially the lads at the back, whose mouths opened further and further and whose cheeks blanched whiter and whiter. Finally,

Benjamin Zephaniah smoothly chatting to a group of streetwise sixth-formers about life on the streets and problems with the police, and then, with fine poetic precision, dropping in a casual reference to Shelley. 'Yeah,' he continued, 'I rate Shelley.' Silence; the listeners brought up short, wide-eyed. Quite without warning, an early-nineteenth-century poet, until then very probably utterly remote from their lives, gained an unexpected credibility.

Three memorable occasions – not least for the students fortunate enough to be present – which were given added support and back-up by having very visible displays of the authors' books brought by the (flexible) bookshop.

For all the talk above about 'anarchy', there is no implication that the visits should not have been thoroughly planned and prepared for, by both writer and school; nor does it mean that the visiting writer or illustrator should have been treated as anything other than a professional. Of course, there were times when the visits did not work; when, for example, either the exigencies of a particular school's curriculum or the lack of interest of a teacher failed to allow sufficient preparation; or when the visiting writer was treated less than adequately. Speaking of the latter, Roger McGough tells of arriving for a school visit, encountering a harassed teacher who had no notion of how to categorise 'a writer' and so made him sit outside the Head's office with all the latecomers! Very much on the other hand is the exemplary attitude of the Head of a First School on the outskirts of Norwich, who opened up the entire school, decorated it *en fête*, invited parents, families, the local bookshop, anyone who was remotely interested, to share in the thrill of a visit by Nick Butterworth to such an extent that he was so impressed – not to say overwhelmed – he found himself unable to leave, and what was originally booked as a single morning session turned into a whole day of shared rejoicing in the sheer joy of books and reading. An occasion in which the Flexible Classroom and the Flexible Bookshop merged seamlessly.

Of course, book events are not only about writers in schools. One weekend, a books-inspired, bookshop-organised event ('happening' would be an apter choice, perhaps) in celebration of Arthur Ransome took place in and around Norwich. Ransome-lovers from all over Britain, as well as some from as far afield as Norway and the United States, gathered together for a diverse programme of events, including talks (one by his biographer, another by his great-nephew); a small exhibition of Ransome memorabilia; an organised coach-tour, supervised and conducted by a local expert on Broadland places associated with the writer, and, as a culmination, a grand regatta on Ranworth Broad, which included film shows in the village hall, teas in the church, a brass band concert and lots of messing about in boats. It rained ceaselessly – and the packed crowds enjoyed it all immensely, not least the local police who had an invigorating time organising the extensive parking arrangements. The success (and it was judged a great success) of the Ransome Weekend brought together many diverse bodies, most of whom had never worked with each other before. These included the Broads Authority, the East Anglian Film Archive, the Norfolk Library Service, the Norfolk Museum Service, the Norfolk Naturalists Trust, Ranworth Church, a boating club calling itself T.A.R.T.S. (yes, quite true) – plus, as overall organiser, the bookshop.

From celebrating an author who loved boating to the contemplation and organisation of a regatta is, taken all in all, nothing more than a basic exercise in lateral thinking. Without it, many opportunities for extending awareness of books can be irretrievably lost. As an example: the touring production of *Junk*, an excellent adaptation of Melvin Burgess's 'controversial' (therefore, momentarily headline-hitting) Carnegie Award-winning novel, played to packed audiences consisting mainly of rapt and ultimately rapturous teenagers. So much so that during one performance a boy was overheard to say, with a distinct air of relief and delight, 'I thought we were coming to see a play by Shakespeare!' (No doubt he was a victim of the M'Choakumchild School of Teaching, and never allowed to catch a glimpse of the plays through the footnotes. But that's another issue.) The point is that this play had really hooked them – and so also may the original book have done. There were, however, no copies on display, no publicity material to announce that there was a book (what was the publisher up to?!), the programme notes made no discernible reference to the existence of a book, let alone that it won the Carnegie! Just a little effort, a smattering of lateral thought, may have made a difference to some – maybe only a few, but that is no matter – of those teenagers.

A final point about book-related events: they do not have to be big, and they need not conform to the received idea of the 'literary' (as opposed to – well what?); the vital factor is to ensure the right book/author/subject for the right audience. One extremely successful event, much less epic than the Ransome Weekend and purely bookshop-based (though it was repeated 'by public demand' soon after in a local school hall) was devoted to Stephan Muthesius' definitive volume on *The English Terraced House*. With the redoubtable author operating the slide projector as well as doing the speaking, it proved to be an evening of erudition, wit, insight and enlightenment. The really important point is that the audience was composed of a cross-section of people – embracing those who could be called 'bookish' and those who under normal circumstances probably rarely entered a book-shop – all brought together by one common bond, the terraced house; either because they lived in one or had previously done so, or purely out of interest to learn more about a familiar aspect of the everyday urban scene. And, should the question arise, a large number of copies of *The English Terraced House* were purchased.

Above all else, a bookshop should strive to be a relaxed environment, in which the public can feel comfortable and unthreatened, staffed by people who have an enthusiasm and knowledge which is entirely free of arrogance. Attempts, at least, should be made to banish the somewhat cloistered air that prevails in some establishments and to encourage them to become more like enticing 'swap-shops' of views, opinions and ideas rather than, as some have been sanctimoniously eulogised, 'temples of culture'(!). And to be – whenever appropriate or necessary – as flexible as possible.

Television and its influence on reading
Stephen Hearst

Background Broadcasting started in the 1920s as a brilliant engineering feat, its possible uses subject to lively debate. Mrs Davidson, wife of the then Archbishop of Canterbury, asked if windows needed to be kept open to let radio waves in. What in essence was this new thing? Would it be a social and cultural or an economic medium? This fundamental question lurked behind every broadcasting policy decision at the time and still does today.

Both Britain and the United States then had, in cultural terms, conservative governments. Yet the decisions made by the two countries in the realm of broadcasting were profoundly different. The Americans, anticipating by 30 years the battle-cry of triumphant corporatism 'what is good for General Motors is good for America', handed radio over to business. In Britain, business, necessary and wealth-creating no doubt, was suspect and money tended to become respectable only in the second and third generation. (Consider the *dramatis personae* in the novels of Evelyn Waugh, Anthony Powell, Dorothy Sayers or P. G. Wodehouse: what most of them have in common is a 'private' income.) So it came about that in Britain the immediate interest group in radio, the manufacturers of radio sets, modestly confined their expectations to the sale of such sets. By 1926, a public corporation set up under a Royal Charter came into being, financed by a licence fee which the users of the emergent radio service were by law compelled to pay. Direction and guidance of radio broadcasting was handed to a tall, stern and assured Scottish engineer, John Reith, who thought out the principles on which this new and revolutionary British cultural activity were to rest in an astonishingly short time. They were: broadcasting in the public interest, public service broadcasting in short; a sense of moral obligation; and assured finance as represented by the licence fee.

Public service broadcasting was to be the public mould for radio and television in Britain for many decades and is likely to go down as the greatest British cultural invention of the twentieth century. In its most uncompromising form it required universality of geographical reception – a feat never achieved in the United States – equality of financial contribution by the user, irrespective of income, and a constant weighing of the public interest by the broadcaster in every programme prior to its transmission. In the event, radio broadcasting soon dispelled most of the doubts voiced by sceptics or by special interests at its birth and became, in the shape of the BBC, an immensely respected national institution.

Television was a different animal altogether. When launched in Britain in

1936 as the first high-definition television service in the world, some of its uses, film for example, were already part of our culture. Yet the Thomases doubting the merits and fearing the consequences of an image-based medium were not just to be found in the community at large, they were perched at the very top of the BBC. 'I regard television as an extension of radio,' was the apocryphal exchange between Sir William Haley, director-general of the BBC, and Norman Collins, controller of the BBC television service. 'And no doubt you regard radio as an extension of the gramophone,' was Collins' rejoinder. He became, in due course, a formidable opponent of the BBC monopoly of broadcasting, as well as a founder member of commercial television. BBC television was kept in fetters; some of its radio masters thought it a passing fad, others saw a visual culture as a threat to language and literature that needed to be contained. The Coronation of Elizabeth II, however, established television as a national as well as a prodigiously growing medium in Britain.

In the United States, broadcasters delivered massive audiences to the advertisers who paid for the broadcasts by giving or claiming to be giving people what they wanted; a free market in broadcasting was not thought all that different from a free market in material goods. To be sure, there was control in the shape of the Federal Communications Commission, but, justified by the First Amendment to the American constitution, virtually every form of broadcasting could be defended as an expression of free speech and its regulation attested as somehow un-American. In Britain, giving people what was known they wanted to see and hear on television seemed an inadequate realisation of their own aims and wishes. Public service broadcasters considered that people could only want what they already knew and that it was their job to widen cultural choices by constantly exploring territory hitherto virgin, as far as the new medium was concerned. Testing these rival assertions by audience research was in its infancy, yet the early 1950s was the only time when fundamental broadcasting issues became a matter of widespread debate: the Churchill government had decided to break the BBC monopoly in broadcasting and to introduce a commercial television channel in the autumn of 1955. This was Britain, remember, not America: competition was meant to be confined to programmes, not to sources of finance. Regulation was tight and franchises were soon withdrawn from contractors who were deemed to have defaulted on their promises and obligations.

The award of a second television channel to the BBC in the 1960s meant that the BBC continued to hold the cultural initiative despite a shrinking financial base. In programme terms Britain in the 1960s and 1970s witnessed an extraordinary flowering of television drama; of science, music and other arts programmes. A very great number of literary classics from Plato to Tolstoy were dramatised and televised. Television, both public and commercial, could, without special pleading, be said to constitute a national theatre. The names of so many contemporary playwrights writing for British Television – Hopkins, Mercer, Potter, Stoppard, Pinter, Frayn, Nicholls, Plater, McGrath, Owen, are only a handful that memory scoops from an abundant well – tended by their work to silence a dwindling band of critics who saw in the dominance of a visual culture grounds of deep foreboding for the future of our language and literature. The commanding heights of British television were, in those years, largely in the hands of producers and directors. Both British and American systems of broadcasting, based on contrasting criteria, could claim to be outstanding success stories, one beyond the forecasts of soothsayers, the other beyond the dreams of avarice. The arrival of Mrs Thatcher at 10 Downing Street changed the premises of British broadcasting. Profound conviction, fortified by radical neo-liberal free market thinking, implanted economic criteria as decisive controls in our broadcasting structure. Programmes became products, accountants took over and disposed.

This brief digest of broadcasting history is a necessary introduction to our theme because we need to distinguish between the features of a visual medium inherent in the technology itself, and the uses to which we put this technology. These uses, in turn, depend on the structures we set up in our democracies to reflect our values and beliefs. And these broadcasting structures come about through the exercise of political and cultural will: political will for government to decide how far laissez faire is to dominate broadcasting policy; cultural will for parents and teachers to influence children over the use of the new media. Public service broadcasting, provided its income is assured for several years ahead, has a duty to be more mindful of the long-term public interest than commercial broadcasting whose cultural offerings depend nowadays to a feverish degree on overnight viewing figures which are acted upon the next morning. Because its finance is predictable and assured, however, it can afford to be more patient, take greater risks and tolerate short-term failure for cultural innovation which needs a longer time-span for public recognition of its merits. (For example, Henry Moore's sculptures were first met by popular incomprehension and ended up, in television terms, as icons of genius.) A profit-based system, even if led by saints, cannot afford the luxury of waiting.) Unfortunately, television can appeal both to the best and the worst in man. Appealing to the best takes longer.

Given this peculiarly British Broadcasting history, what did happen to our reading habits and manners in the television years? Three modes of enquiry suggest themselves: counting, weighing and – guessing.

Some figures
There is no need to join Disraeli in crying 'lies, damned lies and statistics', but our own daily experience surely advises a hefty slab of caution when we quantify our viewing habits and reading. Daily life is not lived in a mansion of rooms, each shut, each with a different label on every door; the doors of ordinary life are open, air flows from room to room and the rods that measure what we do are at best mere warning signals. That said, the figures for television viewing in the United Kingdom, provided by the Office for National Statistics, have been honed over the years to a precision that muffles doubt; what doubt there is might be reserved over the exact cultural consequences of television viewing. Overall, people watched an average of over 25 hours of television a week and listened to just over 16 hours of radio in the United Kingdom in 1995. The corresponding figure for the United States is almost incredible: their television sets are turned on for seven and a half hours each day. (We cannot, of course, tell how much concentrated viewing is taking place.) The weekly British figure for ages 4 to 15 is 16.5 hours for males and 17.14 hours for females. The oldest age group (65 and over), having more free time than their children or grandchildren, watched the most, over 35 hours per week.

Since viewing measurements start with 4-year-olds, it seems appropriate to quote the conclusions of Dutch researchers at Leiden University that, today, children begin to watch television *before* they start to talk, let alone read and that early experiences with this easy and attractive source of entertainment might spoil children's appetite for books later on. The same team concluded that a) elementary school children spend 2.3 hours per day watching television, but on average only 8 minutes per day on leisure-time reading and b) overall, television does have a reductive effect on the book reading of children. However, from Hilde Himmelweit in 1958 to the present day, sociological literary shelves have welcomed and carried new research papers from both Europe and the United States, many of these denying any reductive effect by television on book reading or refraining from uncertain conclusions. Since television viewing figures go up from age group to age group, and no drastic changes in viewing or reading habits might be expected from our 'senior citizens', let us narrow our focus on today's children. Very recent research (1997) undertaken by the London School of Economics Media Research Group on British children aged 6 to

17, concludes that 9 out of 10 children watch television almost every day or every day; that television is identified most often when children are asked which media they would miss most; that television is named most often when children are asked what they talk about with friends; that for parents to 'watch television' represents the most frequent activity they share with their children. And that 'watching television' is identified as the most common leisure activity, from a wide range of activities.

At this point we need to stress the number of what sociologists call 'variables' which complicate all research into possible consequences of television viewing. Indeed the notion of television viewing needs to be refined for, widely available, not merely in wealthy circles are: (1) broadcast television, (2) narrowcast television, (3) pre-recorded video films, (4) films only released on video, (5) video games, (6) interactive video, (7) computer games, (8) camcorders, (9) CD-ROM technology, (10) the Internet, and the latest newcomer – (11) virtual reality. We probably misuse the verb 'add' if we 'add' the pop culture to this list, for pop music figures on videos and CDs. It is a moot question whether time should be added to television viewing figures to accommodate the phenomenal popularity of this medium among the young – and not so young. (No statistics are at present available as to how much leisure time is taken up by listening to pop music, viewing pop videos or disco visits.) A recent edition of *The Economist* recorded that British pop music contributes more in export earnings than the British Steel industry, and that domestic music sales reached 1.7 billion in 1996, which means that Britain spends more on pop music than on fruit and vegetables. The LSE Media Group research also points to the use of a relatively new phenomenon, termed the bedroom culture. Children up to 9 years of age watch television in family spaces, whereas 46 per cent of 13 to 14-year-olds were found to enjoy watching television alone. It would appear that more and more teenagers convert their bedrooms into multiple-media laboratories which they tend to share with their own friends. Parents' fears for their children's safety, in terms of the drugs menace and of traffic dangers, reinforce this trend; and we must add to these fears the lack of other available safe, publicly-funded facilities.

Surveys of reading habits in Britain, while not differing greatly in their quantitative estimates, are all wrapped in caution and for good reason. Qualitative criteria can easily creep into figures that, on the face of it, look coldly objective, but can easily be interpreted in divergent ways. For example, the percentage of people reading daily national newspapers has fallen consistently since 1981: from 76 per cent to 62 per cent in 1995 for men, from 68 per cent to 54 per cent in 1995 for women, whereas the total num-

ber of book titles published in the United Kingdom has gone up year by
year from 35,608 in 1975 to 101,504 in 1996. So caveats need to be
quickly entered: it appears that a larger proportion of people, about two-
thirds, read national Sunday newspapers rather than daily ones in 1995 to
1996. And, as to book titles, they do not tell us the number of individual
titles printed or sold. Some titles are printed in minute quantities, others in
hundreds of thousands. Other figures are less controversial. Over half of
people aged 15 and over held a library ticket in 1995. The total number of
books borrowed from public libraries in 1994 to 1995 was over 550 million – some 100 million *fewer* than in 1981 to 1982. Seven out of 10 people
borrowing books in 1994 also used other facilities, such as sound and video
recordings. The 10 most borrowed adult authors in 1994 to 1995 were
Catherine Cookson, Danielle Steel, Dick Francis, Ruth Rendell, Agatha
Christie, Ellis Peters, Jack Higgins, Wilbur Smith, Virginia Andrews and
Terry Pratchett, whilst the most sought-after children's authors were Janet
and Allen Ahlberg, Roald Dahl and Enid Blyton.

In terms of expenditure, book purchases in local authority libraries
declined between 1989 to 1990 and 1994 to 1995, while audio-visual
acquisitions went up. Estimated domestic sales of United Kingdom publishers between 1985 and 1994 *increased* in real terms (at constant 1990
prices) by 21.6 per cent in all three listed categories (consumer books,
school books and academic/professional books). The same figures, *unad-
justed* for inflation, show a doubling of sales for school books from £87
million in 1985 to £177 million in 1994, while consumer books went from
£619 million to £1,128 million and academic/professional books from
£242 million to £451 million. Most recent statistics on the book-buying
public divided into light buyers who buy between one and three books per
year, medium buyers who acquire four to nine books per year and heavy
buyers who buy 10 or more books per year. It is interesting to note that
between 1993 and 1995, heavy buyers accounted for between 73 and 79
per cent of book purchases.

Retail book outlets now comprise the following categories: books/sta-
tionery shops, bookshops, bargain bookshops, confectioners, tobacconists
and newsagents, supermarkets, chain stores, stations and airports, gift
shops and schools/colleges. A final figure: as a percentage of consumer
spending on books, the United Kingdom spends 0.364 per cent of gross
domestic product, less than France (0.376 per cent) and Germany (0.440
percent), but more than the United States (0.353 per cent). A rush to judge-
ment is perhaps premature. Yet even cautious weighing of these figures con-
jures up Juvenal's dictum '*Nemo repente fuit turpissimus*' (no-one ever

reached the climax of vice at one step). Image *is* driving language from some of the commanding heights of cultural influence, to sounds of popular approbation.

Some arguments

A scrutiny of what television does to reading ought to consider what this visual medium does well and what it does badly. For nearly five decades it has, for millions of viewers, acted as entertainer, teacher, information service, documentary-maker, circus, sports witness and promotion, journalist, creator and interpreter of artistic endeavours, music-maker and interpreter, church, presence at State occasions, even confessor of some of the most intimate details of our private lives. It would be absurd to claim that the medium does all these things equally well. Yet, over the years, most leading television spokesmen have emphatically denied that television influences views on behaviour, that its violent episodes are imitated in real life, that television can conceivably do actual harm. Television's disclaimer on influence is virtually untenable, since advertisers spend their billions on which the whole of commercial television depends in the precise knowledge that their messages *do* influence people. When it comes to defending what television does its practitioners adopt the tactics of the British Army in the Sudan towards the end of the nineteenth century: they form squares and shoot outwards. A succession of visual images, backed in a large number of programmes by music, evokes emotions, but is not a natural source of clear thought.

For reason to flourish we need man's supreme achievement on his evolutionary path to *Homo sapiens*, language. Pictures work supremely well as symbols and expressions of our deepest feelings, but language is the indispensable tool in the exercise of reason, in the precise expression of thought. The need to state the obvious is itself a symptom of how images have taken over ground precisely held by language. And in a mature democracy, where every vote carries equal weight, the achievement of critical literacy, the ability to judge and weigh the truth or falsity of things, is not merely desirable, it is of the essence. Television, a combination of visual and linguistic signals, endeavours to serve a host of disciplines, often allowing one or the other of their signals the upper hand. In the discussion of political issues, for instance, it must largely confine itself to what professionals have dismissively called talking heads. In the selection and positioning of news items, a balance is constantly struck between their visual potential and their ability to convey new information. Nothing exposes the comparative impotence of a visual medium in this sphere of politics more clearly than the daily pic-

tures of the exterior of ministries over which the text of policy pronounce-
ments is superimposed: to make sense you need language. Hence, the more
we read off our screens, the less the danger of our being overwhelmed, confused or befuddled by images. Yet the images count: political commenta-
tors all rush to be seen against the door of 10 Downing Street, although
they get their inside knowledge by phone or fax.

In stark contrast, natural history has found in television a wonderful
means of representation, since its astounding camera work can now register the minutest details of animal behaviour. The same is largely true of
most science programmes as a great deal of scientific evidence relies on
visual observation. At the opposite end of televisual suitability we have philosophy and religion. It has been some time since we saw philosophers discussing philosophy and if it ever happens again we will probably be invited
to record it off air in the small hours. As to religion: soaring pillars, splendidly lit architraves, singing congregations, but hardly any mention or discussion of theology. If theology is not at the heart of religion, what is?
Somewhere in between these opposed 'poles' lies the realm of history. Well
served for periods, coinciding with the invention of photography, and brilliantly successful when viewers are witnessing fateful decisions (as in the
break-up of the Yugoslav federation), any account of classical Roman or
Greek history is confined to stone, marble and the authority of the presen-
ter, making the reading of Edward Gibbon all the more desirable.

Some of British television's most celebrated accomplishments lie in the
dramatic serial adaptations of the novels of Charles Dickens, Jane Austen
and George Eliot. Narrative drive, a very prominent characteristic of English writing, has leapt successfully from page to screen, because the question 'What happened next' satisfies the curiosity of readers and viewers
alike. (This is not the case in Germany, whose writers tend to prefer asking
'What is the problem here?'; hence the writing of thrillers is, in general, in
Anglo-Saxon hands.) Moreover, these dramatisations stimulate a demand
for the original books, as booksellers, librarians and publishers attest.
What they cannot achieve, however, is to render these great writers full justice. The irony of Jane Austen evaporates under the sight of stately car-
riages and homes; the moral insights of George Eliot are excised by the loss
of the author's voice and lines. Dickens's readings in vision are the closest
we can possibly get to the real Dickens prose, not the visual substitutions
achieved by casting and scenery in prestigious productions. Great language
can be successfully translated into other languages, but cries out to be read
in the original when transposed in sound and vision. Nevertheless, if these
adaptations return us to the library or bookshop they must be reckoned as

much among the countervailing forces to a spread of viewing at the expense of reading, as are the phenomenal increases in university education and adult education.

But there lies another charge against the consequence of television viewing – its speed of transmission. Reading, a dialogue between writer and reader, proceeds at the reader's own speed. Television broadcasting, however, has until recently entered our conscious understanding at the broadcaster's speed (the video recorder now enables us to stop and turn back, just as we can turn back a page in a book). This broadcasting speed has steadily increased over the years; look at 30-year-old programmes and see how slow many of them seem to us today. (Commercials, filling the costliest television seconds or minutes, have almost reached subliminal haste.) The consequences of this electronic speeding-up process are at least as great as any measurable replacement of reading by viewing: the attention span of the viewer, particularly the young viewer, is being shortened by an ever-quickening delivery of pictures. Add the new channels brought by cable and satellite as well as the outlets we listed earlier on, all instantly conjured up at the touch of a zapper, and the observations of researchers reporting that some children find school dull compared with the fun they get out of television make a good deal of sense. There is no need, though, to despair as monks did painting incunabula when printing was invented and gradually put them out of business.

Some guesses and conclusions
Digital broadcasting makes hundreds of television channels possible and will change the relationship of broadcaster and viewer. There will be broadcasters addressing fragmented, hence smaller, audiences; narrowcasters speaking to specific interest groups; audiences choosing what to view at a time of their own choosing; multiple uses of the television screen; and the role of the viewer will change from recipient to being a possible correspondent whose reaction to certain programmes will be eagerly sought and who will also be enabled to start, stop, rewind and to agree or disagree, as with the author of a book. Cultural forecasts are notoriously prone to fall victim to the stubborn tendency of life to appear in shapes and sizes we haven't dreamt of. Hundreds of possible channels will induce pessimists to intone Shakespeare's 'When sorrows come, they come not single spies, but in battalions', while optimists will conjure up an electronic Shangri-la where the wise and the foolish, the teacher and the taught are 'wired up' together, in harmony of course. Already available technology, however, does allow the cautious punter to place some fairly safe bets. Passive, seemingly effortless

television viewing, as portrayed by Neil Postman and other doomsday prophets, will still be possible, but face a challenge from the Internet's keyboard. We are all likely to be consulted on our views by cultural or political interests. Some of our reading will be transferred from the printed page to the electronic screen. Why heave volumes of the *Encyclopaedia Britannica* off crowded shelves when all its contents can be punched up from a single CD-ROM? To be sure, no technology can by itself ensure the spread of critical literacy, but the sheer fun of finding things out for oneself is likely to make a difference to the character and the quality of our cultural pursuits. A transfer of initiative, from broadcaster to narrowcaster, coupled with a computer-driven awareness of what I, Citizen Smith, will be able to do at the touch of a few buttons, can restore what present-day television is accused of taking away: one's right to absorb information at one's own speed; the potential to say 'Hold on a bit, let me think this out for myself'. Digital broadcasting raises further possibilities: channels for book reviews, discussions and readings which could be run cheaply by publishing or literary interests, electronic bookshops and access to reference libraries through the Internet. Paying for these services will cost a multiple of the present licence fee, but millions of people are willing to pay such sums for live football already and may be persuaded to look upon electronic 'extras' as life-enhancing. A judicious continuation of such channels with the Internet (which requires extensive reading) offers hope, to put it no higher, that our language and its critical usage will not be submerged. Over 50 years ago, a retiring BBC mandarin concluded her valedictory address with these words: 'I hope you will make television so good that people won't have to watch it any more'. Her hopes were dashed partly because broadcasting from the few to the many did not demand much effort from the latter. The new technology does.

Yet all these hopes are based on premises we can no longer take for granted: namely that digital broadcasting is *bound* to usher in greater cultural choice and that public service broadcasting will continue. Digital broadcasting will certainly fragment audiences without making the cost of an hour's drama or documentary any cheaper: theirs are fixed with constantly mounting costs, amounting to over half a million pounds for drama per hour and well over £100,000 per hour for documentaries. Only large-scale operators can afford such costs and the likelihood must be that digital operations for high-quality television productions will be concentrated in fewer and fewer private hands. In a multi-media world, public service television can only survive by the exertion of political will in safeguarding public service broadcasting institutions by the spending of public money.

In Britain, public money is represented by a licence fee tied to the retail price index. Unfortunately, broadcasting is labour intensive (80 percent of the BBC's income is spent on fees and salaries), and labour costs have always risen faster than the basket of goods making up the Retail Price Index. The result for at least two decades has been that the financial gap between Britain's public and commercial television sector has become very large. If public service broadcasting were to shrink or disappear altogether – a very real possibility – the cultural consequences would be hard to exaggerate and they include the threats to reading represented by purely populist forms of programming. Public service broadcasting recognises that we are all at times part of cultural majorities, at other times of cultural minorities. Philosophers have been known to be sports enthusiasts; taxi drivers have won national general knowledge contests. Commercial broadcasting cannot afford to wait for novel or unexpected artifacts to take root and must always endeavour to reinforce existing taste. An entirely commercial broadcasting system, moreover, must compete even more fiercely for the same advertising revenue, with the almost certain consequence that programme standards will suffer. Public service broadcasting, its income guaranteed, must seek to make good programmes popular and popular programmes good. It must seek a higher aim than to interpret the public interest as that which interests the public. A mixed public service and commercial broadcasting system, each strong enough not to drive the other out of business, is, therefore, a highly desirable characteristic of the coming digital broadcasting age. What we see, hear or read on the screens in the future will depend on the policies for electronic communication we legislate into being. Hitherto, we have shown no noticeable interest in such policies. Unless we do, we may come to regret that we did not stand up and be counted.

References

Beentjes, Johannes W. J. and van der Vont, Tom H. A. (1988), *Television's Impact on Children's Reading Skills: a review of Research* (Leiden University)

Briggs, Asa (1961–95), *The History of Broadcasting in the United Kingdom,* 6 vols (Oxford University Press)

Graham, Andrew and Davies, George (1997), *Broadcasting, Society and Policy in the Multimedia Age* (Luton University Press)

Himmelweit, Hilde, Oppenheim, A. N. and Vince, P. (1958), *Television and the Child* (London: Oxford University Press)

Kirby, Robert and Csikszentmikalyi, Mikaly (1990), *Television and the Quality of Life: How Viewing Shapes Everyday Experience* (Hillsdale, NJ: Lawrence Erlbaum Associates)

Koolstine, Cees M., van der Vont, Tom H. A. and van der Kemp, Leo J. Th. (1997) *Television's Impact on Children's Reading Comprehension and Decoding Skills: A 3-year Panel Study* (Leiden University)

LSE Media Research Group (1997), *Children, Young People and Changing Media Environment* (co-ordinated by Dr Sonia Livingstone and Dr George Gaskell)

Postman, Neil (1982), *The Disappearance of Childhood* (New York: Delacarte Press)
Cultural Trends, No. 26, 1995 Edition (Office for National Statistics, London: The Stationery Office)

The Economist, Volume 345, Issue 8048

Social Trends, No. 27, 1997 Edition (Office for National Statistics, London: The Stationery Office)

Part 3 Reading education

Those of us who argue for creativity to have a greater role do so because of the overwhelming evidence that allowing expressiveness and imaginative curiosity to flourish creates a level of confidence, self-esteem and purposefulness that can change a child's abilities for ever.
Jude Kelly, Director, West Yorkshire Playhouse

Modernising Britain is about improving basic literacy and numeracy but it is also about encouraging the imagination and creativity that will form the key resources in the most successful economies.
Diane Coyle, Independent (February 1998)

Reading is much more than the decoding of black marks upon a page: it is a quest for meaning and one which requires the reader to be an active participant.
The Cox Report (1989)

National Curriculum terms

PRIMARY	SECONDARY	
Key Stage 1 *Years: Reception, 1 and 2* *Age 4 to 7*	Key Stage 3 *Years: 7 to 9* *Ages 11 to 14*	
Key Stage 2 *Years: 3 to 6* *Ages 7 to 11*	Key Stage 4 (GCSE) *Years: 10 to 11* *Ages 14 to 16*	A Level/GNVQ *Years: 12 to 13*

Pupils are tested at the end of each Key Stage by nationally administered tests up to the end of Key Stage 3. GCSE and A Level are still administered by competing boards, but at GCSE the syllabi have to conform to the national curriculum. Although A Level is not covered by the National Curriculum, all syllabi have to conform to guidelines set by the same authority, the Qualification and Curriculum Authority.

Other terms and references

The National Literacy Strategy: Framework for Teaching is a folder given to all primary schools. It comes from the Standards and Effectiveness Unit, a sub-section of the DfEE, and is a creation of the Labour government. It is intended for use in the 'Literacy Hour' – this, too, is a recommendation of the Standards and Effectiveness Unit in which all children, for an hour a day, use the materials provided for in *The National Literacy Strategy*.

In theory all this is voluntary, the *Strategy* only guidelines, but in reality all but a handful will be implementing the 'Literacy Hour' as schools are required to prove that their method is better, to justify non-compliance with *The National Literacy Strategy*.

English teachers and the third way
Bethan Marshall

My young friends, I am very grieved to tell you that if you have to come up to Oxford with the idea of getting knowledge you must give that up at once ... The curriculum is designed on the idle plan that all of the knowledge will be found inside the covers of four Latin and four Greek books, though not the same four each year ... A genuine love of learning is one of the two delinquencies which cause blindness and lead a young man to ruin
   Stoppard

The bleak spectre of utilitarianism hangs over our schools like a pall. As we approach the millennium Gradgrind has the upper hand and the Government is on his side. Document after document, guidelines, frameworks, policy statements issue forth from the various government agencies and they all amount to much the same thing. Facts are what they want and the certainty that goes with them. There is one way of learning to read – via the Literacy Framework – and one reason for doing it – to enhance our economic performance. The profound unease with which these developments have been greeted at every level by those involved in the teaching of English, from infant class to university department, is reflected in the essays that follow in this section. But to understand the issues that they discuss, we need to consider how we have arrived at this position, a mere 10 years after the Conservatives began to devise a national curriculum for schools in England and Wales.

   In the beginning, there appeared to be room for debate. Margaret Thatcher may have wanted a curriculum where the basics were spelled out, but those involved in the writing of the documents took a different view and initially they got their way. They wished to produce an entitlement curriculum for all pupils. The notion of an entitlement curriculum goes well beyond the scope of one which simply describes a set of skills that need to be acquired; it considers what you would need to know, understand and appreciate to be educated in that subject and then demands that all pupils have access to such a curriculum.

   In 1989, Professor Brian Cox was given the unenviable task of chairing the working party that would eventually produce the first national curriculum for English. Unique, however, among all subsequent documents produced by both Conservative and Labour governments on any aspect of the English curriculum, including literacy, in schools, and for initial teacher training, Brian Cox's working party admitted that there was debate about

English. In his report, which preceded the publication of the curriculum, Professor Cox and his colleagues, most notably Katherine Perera, famously acknowledged that there were different 'views' of the subject. They listed five and gave them the following headings – cultural heritage, adult needs, cross curricular, personal growth and cultural analysis (DES and WO, 1989, para. 2.20–27, p. 21).

It was not their aim, however, to be divisive. In what became known as *The Cox Report*, they were adamant that the views 'were not to be seen as sharply distinguishable, and certainly not mutually exclusive' (DES and WO, 1989, para. 2.20) and in his book *Cox on Cox*, Brian Cox explains the rationale behind the acknowledgement that there is no neatly defined view of the subject. 'This list is of vital importance, for it gives a broad approach to the curriculum which can unite the profession' (Cox, 1991 p. 21).

And this is precisely what it achieved. Andrew Goodwyn of Reading University surveyed English teachers on their allegiance to the five views for an article in the journal *English in Education* (Goodwyn, 1992). He discovered that the majority of teachers subscribed to a 'personal growth' view of the subject; a substantial minority were cultural analysts, and that there was little support for the other views as the main aim or purpose of their teaching. Yet all who were surveyed were broadly sympathetic to the curriculum as a whole and many felt that their practice had been enhanced and broadened by the process.

What Cox and his working party had done, by acknowledging differences, was to allow teachers room for manoeuvre. In the true liberal tradition, the curriculum reminded teachers that there were other viewpoints that needed to be recognised, but gave them scope to interpret these views from their own position. In other words, if, as a teacher, you believed that the personal growth of your pupils was your aim, the canon of literature became a vehicle for achieving this. Preparing children for the world of work became a by-product rather than a specific focus. On the other hand, for the cultural analyst the canon became an example of the way in which society invests certain iconic texts with power, so pushing other groups to the margin; personal growth depends on an increased understanding of such processes and the ability to think critically, which in turn prepares children for their life as adults. The idea that English teachers should strive to create pupils who could express themselves effectively was so obvious within the profession that it almost went without saying; so too was the realisation that this was often difficult to achieve.

Yet the choice of views that *The Cox Report* identified goes some way to understanding why his curriculum was so quickly undermined by the Conservatives and why so much of it still finds little support under Labour. Within three years of its introduction the Tories began to re-write the national curriculum for English, this time under the leadership of David Pascal, a chemical engineer and associate of the right-wing think tank the Centre for Policy Studies.

Strongly held beliefs and fears coalesce around the views of 'cultural heritage', 'adult needs' and the 'cross curricular' that have made them the focus of public debate and anxiety in the way in which the other two have not. For it is these three views, rather than the other two – 'personal growth' and 'cultural analysis' – that form the basis of any discussion about standards and, more particularly, the way in which they are always described in terms of their decline.

The notion of 'cultural heritage' was of particular concern to the Conservatives and they gave this view a very distinct spin. The Cox curriculum insisted that pre-twentieth-century literature should be studied but only named one author – Shakespeare. For many within the Party and in society at large, however, the subject of English had became the repository of Englishness, a reality that they saw under threat. The revised curriculum, written by David Pascal and his working party, sought to protect us from the spectre of that fractured cultural hegemony by the inclusion of a literary canon to be studied, which would transmit the values of society which they wished to convey. As Eliot wrote in 1948, in *Notes Towards a Definition of Culture*: 'There is the question of what culture is, and the question whether it is anything we can control or deliberately influence. These questions confront us whenever we devise a theory, or frame a policy, of education' (Eliot, 1975, p. 294).

And, like the Tories, he went on to warn of the dangers of cultural disintegration and looked to education as a way of shoring the crumbling citadel. Edward Said, in his book *Culture and Imperialism*, spells out the sub-text of such an approach: 'In time, culture comes to be associated, often aggressively, with the nation or the state; this differentiates 'us' from 'them', almost always with some degree of xenophobia' (Said, 1993, p. xiii).

While English teachers were happy to introduce children to canonical writers because of the quality of their writing, few could support such an agenda and they protested vigorously. This fight coincided with a boycott of national curriculum tests, and although this, too, was spearheaded by English teachers, for reasons that are explored in depth by John Wilks and Anne Barnes below, it was implemented by the unions, and so became a fight less about education and more about pay and conditions. With the ignominious resignation of the Conservative Secretary of State for Education, John Patten, the Tories looked to an honest broker to clean up the mess. Enter Sir Ron Dearing of the Post Office and another re-write of the curriculum.

Pascal's curriculum never saw the light of day, but the legacy of his canon stayed on under Sir Ron. While the overall tone of his curriculum was less little Englander, the restrictive effects of it, particularly at GCSE, are described, in Anne Barnes' essay.

Labour's fixation with declining standards has had less to do with culture and more to do with the 'adult needs' and 'cross curricular' views identified in *The Cox Report*, though, even here, the antecedents of their preoccupation lie with the Conservatives and beyond. Almost from the beginning of public education, standards have apparently been falling. In 1912, a head teacher wrote to *The Times* complaining that 'Reading Standards are falling because parents no longer read to their children and too much time is spent listening to the gramophone' (cited, Cox, 1995, p. 37). In the same year the English Association wrote that, 'It is a plain fact that the average girl or boy is unable to write English with a clearness or fluency or any degree of grammatical accuracy (ibid., p. 37). *The Newbolt Report* in 1921 concluded that, 'The teaching of English in present day schools produces a very limited command of the English language' (ibid., p. 37). In the same report all but a few employers complained 'often bitterly' (ibid., p. 37) that they had found difficulty in 'obtaining employees who can speak and write English clearly and correctly... spelling in particular received adverse comment' (ibid., p. 38). Seven years later little had changed. *The Spens Report* of 1928 wrote, 'It is a common and grave criticism that many pupils pass through grammar school without acquiring the capacity to express themselves in English' (ibid., p. 38). *The Norwood Report* of 1943 claimed to have received 'strong evidence of the poor quality of English of Secondary School pupils ... the evidence is such as to leave no doubt in our minds that we are confronted by a serious failure of secondary schools' (ibid., p. 38). With such a catalogue of doom it is a wonder that any of us can read and write at all.

There is a sense, however, in which all politicians of whatever persuasion foster such a crisis, for without a crisis there is no problem to be solved, no firm leadership to be taken. But the debate goes beyond this. For what needs to be recognised is that, for some, a split infinitive is the equivalent of a moral lapse; that the standard in standard English is as much about standards of behaviour as it is about a linguistic code. Again, this fear of the moral consequences of falling standards was given its clearest articulation under the Conservative government. It was Norman Tebbit who remarked in an interview on the *Today* programme, in 1985, 'If you allow standards to slip to the stage where good English is no better than bad English, where people can turn up filthy and nobody takes any notice of them at school – just as well as turning up clean – all those things tend to cause people to have no standards at all, and once you lose your standards then there's no imperative to stay out of crime.'

Yet such a view was not only given credence by Tory ministers. John Rae, the former head teacher at Westminster School, while making the link less crudely causal, also sees an explicit connection between the permissive society and progressive teaching: 'The overthrow of grammar coincided with the acceptance of the equivalent of creative writing in social behaviour. As nice points of grammar were mockingly dismissed as pedantic and irrelevant, so was punctiliousness in such matters as honesty, responsibility, property, gratitude, apology and so on' (*Observer*, February 1982).

Given the prevalence of such views, for the Labour politician, arguments about literacy have to have the same totem effect as law and order. They, too, have to be tough on poor spelling and the causes of poor spelling. But Labour has added a new dimension to the debate. Their first year in office has been characterised by a desire to be in control and on message. No deviation from the party line has been brooded, no dissenting voice can be heard. And they have carried this approach into education policy. Their rationale has been that we need a highly literate work force to carry us into the hi-tech future of the millennium. On the back of this uncontroversial statement they have introduced, under the thinly disguised veil of non-compulsory guidance, the single most prescriptive set of policies that this country has ever seen. The nature of the Literacy Strategy is discussed in Henrietta Dombey's insightful essay on that document below. Its shortcomings are passionately described by Margaret Meek in hers.

These two writers, along with all the others in this section, speak with a voice that comes from traditions very different from that of new Labour; ones that Professor Brian Cox and his working party remembered but that the politicians either forgot or actively sought to oppose. It was Matthew Arnold who first espoused the view that teaching literature had the capacity to transform; that Art and aesthetic sensibility were central to the liberal imagination. His legacy is found in Judy Simons' survey of university English departments (below), the place where most English teachers start to form their judgements about the subject, and, where the English teachers that inspired them to teach will have begun to formulate their ideas also.

Alongside this tradition exists the notion of critical dissent; that society and its norms are there to be analysed and challenged; that critical thinking should be fostered and encouraged. And it is these two latter views that have dominated school English over the last 40 years and been evident from the very beginning of public education – from Brian Cox, via James Britten, to F. R. Leavis and back to Arnold himself. Some have emphasised the radical, others the liberal, but all to a person have opposed the utilitarian as the dominant view of their subject. Shift the paradigm away from a skills view of the subject towards seeing English as an Art and all else changes with it, not least the way in which it can be assessed.

Since 1992, the chief complaint of English teachers has been about the way in which the subject is assessed and the dangers of teaching to the test. In essence their arguments are no different from those of Matthew Arnold writing nearly 150 years ago. For, as he wrote in 1867, 'By ingenious preparation (as it is now found possible) to get children through the Revised Code examination in reading writing and ciphering, without their really knowing how to read write or cipher, so it will in practice, no doubt be found possible to get three fourths of the one fifth of the children over six through the examination in grammar, geography, and history, without their really knowing any one of these three matters' (Arnold, 1979, p.96).

Two years later he saw no change. 'All test examinations ...' he complained, 'may be said to narrow reading upon a certain given point, and to make it mechanical' (ibid., p. 95). He went on to warn of the dangers of teaching to the test when the stakes were high, for the school grant depended on the pupils' success in the test: 'It tends to make instruction mechanical and to set a bar to duly extending it ... [and] must inevitably concentrate the teachers' attention on producing this minimum and not simply on the good instruction of the school. The danger to be guarded against is the mistake of assuming these two – the producing of the minimum successfully and the good instruction of the school – as if they were identical' (ibid., p. 95).

He could be Terry Furlong or John Wilks, Anne Barnes or Jane Ogborn and, like theirs, his warnings should be heeded. More children passing the tests, particularly at Key Stage 2, which is the narrowest of them all, does not necessarily mean an increase in literacy. It may simply mean that teachers have got better at getting children through the hoops. And that will almost certainly entail making 'instruction mechanical' and have little to do with 'the good instruction of the school'.

But, when contemplating the Literacy Hour, perhaps we should leave the last word to Katherine Bathurst, an Inspector for the Board of Education in 1905, who wrote on the need for national nurseries. She describes, from a new boy's point of view, a scenario which may once again become eerily familiar:

A blackboard has been produced, and hieroglyphics are drawn upon it by the teacher. At a given signal every child in the class begins calling out mysterious sounds: 'Letter A, letter A' in a sing-song voice, or 'Letter A says Ah, letter A says Ah', as the case may be. To the uninitiated I may explain that No. 1 is the beginning of spelling, and No. 2 is the beginning of word building. Hoary-headed men will spend hours discussing whether 'c-a-t" or "ker-ar-te' are the best means of conveying the knowledge of how to read 'cat'. I must own an indifference to the point myself, and sympathise with teachers not allowed to settle it for themselves.

She goes on to describe the way in which the process is repeated for the letter B: *This occupation lasts perhaps twenty minutes, but of this our baby has no knowledge; it is many many years since he left the delicious liberty and enchanting variety of the gutter. The many coloured world has changed into a monotonous hue, and people say one thing so many times it makes him sleepy. 'Wake up, Johnny; it's not time to go to sleep yet. Be a good boy and watch teacher'* (Van der Eyken, 1973, p.121)

Literacy is not enough.

References

Arnold, M. (1979), *Selected Poetry and Prose*, ed. Denys Thompson (London: Heinemann)

Bathurst, K. (1905),'The need for national nurseries', *Nineteenth Century and After* (London: Penguin)

Cox B. (1991), *Cox on Cox* (London: Hodder and Stoughton)

Cox B. (1995), *Cox on the Battle for the English Curriculum* (London: Hodder and Stoughton)

DFE and WO (1993), *English for Ages 5–16* (London: HMSO)

DfEE (1995), *English in the National Curriculum* (London: HMSO)

DES and WO. (1989), 'English for ages 5–16', *The Cox Report* (London: HMSO)

DES and the WO. (1990), *English in the National Curriculum* (London: HMS0)

Goodwyn, A. (1992), 'English teachers and the Cox models' (*English and Education*, Vol. 26, Issue 3)

Kermode, F. (ed.) (1975), 'Notes towards a definition of culture', *Selected Prose of T. S. Eliot* (London: Faber and Faber)

Said, E. (1993), *Culture and Imperialism* (London: Chatto and Windus)

Stoppard, T. (1997), *The Invention of Love* (London: Faber and Faber)

Van der Eyken, W. (ed.) (1973), *Education, The Child and Society: A Documentary History 1900–1973*

Important reading lessons
Margaret Meek

The imaginative transformation of human life is the means by which we
can most truly grasp and comprehend it
  Seamus Heaney

No government promises full, rich literacy for all. Perhaps the Literacy
Task Force, aware of increasing evidence of fundamental changes in communication systems and the need to 'transform literacy standards', came as
near as it dared in declaring that the new education service should do
'whatever it takes' to ensure that all children are taught to read *well* by age
11, 'as the first step towards the creation of a truly literate nation and a pre-
requisite of a learning society'. [1] Given such statements of intent, no one
with any sense could quarrel with the expressed desire to bring about a
'dramatic improvement' in children's reading and writing. The trouble with
the texts of official educational documents is that they exemplify the kind
of literacy they are to promote: management prose to plan and regulate
affairs, no nonsense, no argument, no loopholes. This became clear in the
revisions of the National Curriculum Orders for English. Now, instead of
being encouraged to demonstrate the relation of reading and writing to
new communication systems and modern literature, teachers are overwhelmed by old-fashioned instructions, as cut and dried as anything proposed by the government inspector in *Hard Times*.

My scepticism about claims for the effective teaching of reading as, predominantly, repeated exercises in comprehension, grammar and spelling,
comes from working with and observing highly professional teachers
whose focus is on children learning to read and recording how they do it.
They do not underestimate any child's ability to make sense of texts
designed to be read in a context which promotes understanding. By choosing reading matter for its significance and value, collecting samples of children's interactions with texts, linking writing and reading across the entire
curriculum, they demonstrate the power and potential of literate behaviour
and the actual satisfaction of learning to read and write. Where the learners
have a rich experience of texts, they successfully acquire phonological
awareness, contextual, grammatical and graphic knowledge; they orches-
trate these textual features with their understanding of language and life.
All these aspects of early reading challenge the notion that, in children's
growth as literates, there is a predictable, uniform, sequential programme
of lessons which ensures success.

As the result of studying 'readerly' behaviour in both teachers and pupils,

I am convinced that what children read plays a vital role in all their book learning, their anticipation of success and the effortful practice that all skills require. Good readers read a lot of what they like. Given encouragement, they branch out to new texts from familiar ones. Their experience gives them confidence to understand the different patterning of sentences, the variables of syntax and the fact that words often mean more than they say. Desire to be able to read does not begin with the discovery of patterns of rhyme in nursery verses but, instead, follows the sheer delight in being able to recite them and to see them in books with pictures, over and over again. Sadly, there is still a fairly general assumption that texts which exemplify what reading can be like are the reward for learning to read, rather than the means by which readers are made, right from the beginning.

Parents are now aware of the implications of 'a good start', so children learn important reading lessons before school. The National Literacy Trust has made this a priority area. Its database records more than 1,000 preschool initiatives where adults and children read together. Libraries make special borrowing arrangements to help adults extend the range of their familiarity with children's books. These early reading events are allied to children's dramatic play and play with words. Well-known tales teach predictable narrative conventions, structures and devices. Hints of secrecy, knowing what is meant but not said, lurk in the literary lore children trade with each other, as Peter and Iona Opie made plain.[2] There are also deeper attractions, seductions even, in children's early texts to pull the readers back and back to books like David McKee's *Not Now Bernard*. These are the actuality of feelings which, as yet, they have no words for.

The most famous of these texts, Maurice Sendak's classic *Where the Wild Things Are,* has only 338 words. In conjunction with the richly-detailed artwork, the story is shaped and paced into a drama of aggression and reconciliation. When beginners insist on reading by themselves 'and it was still hot', the words on the last page, they are responding to more than the temperature of Max's supper. They have just seen the images of Max grow ever bigger as the story proceeded. He gazed at them twice, directly from the page. Now they are glad, and relieved, that he finds home more desirable than being king of all the monsters. The textuality of the whole book 'says something' utterly significant, total, worth exploring further. The text remains the same for each re-reading, so readers discover more about it, with and without adult help.

Children who are read to have reading experiences beyond their ability to read. Book language reappears in conversations and in children's games. In their own versions of stories children explore, intellectually, the nature of their own situation – childhood. In pointing out the unique contribution of children's literature to these explorations, Peter Hollindale says that the texts that authors and artists make for young readers enrich and diversify their sense of what it is to be a child both in itself and as a stage en route to being something else.[3] While listening to stories, children enter the realms of possibility; what might happen, how things could be different. As they gradually learn to become both the teller and the told, the absolutely crucial reading lesson, they are also learning to dialogue with their futures. When we examine this evidence in conjunction with the history of children's literature in English and the new stories that come to us from other cultures, it seems extraordinary that this body of texts, in all its diversity, is still not prominently part of the mainstream teaching of reading in England. True, some reading schemes have adopted newer styles of production and a broader range of texts, but many schools still depend on teaching books designed as particular lessons for 'doing reading', and their pupils are not invited to sample the rich literature which is undoubtedly theirs to learn from.

To understand that artists and authors now create texts for primary schoolchildren which give them a vision of what reading can be like in terms of what Gunther Kress calls 'the child's own semiotic disposition',[4] we have to side-step the current rhetoric of school reading lessons. It is fairly straightforward to share modern children's books with teachers already skilled in reading them, but it is difficult to explain the important features of individual books to those who have never looked closely at a new picture book – *Cloudland* by John Burningham, for example – nor taken seriously the work of skilled artists, writers and publishers who invent new texts for new readers. One distinctive feature of these is 'dual address', whereby an author like Anthony Browne intrigues both the helping adult and the learner. To make the best use of the best that is produced for children to read, adults have to be convinced that young people, not only beginners, need access to more texts than they can read for themselves.

Picture books are the distinctive medium for children's early reading. The economics of world distribution of illustrated pages mean that the multiple formats of Raymond Briggs' *The Snowman* are available in many languages. English readers have a choice of different formats and versions. In expressing their preferences, even quite young readers make detailed comparisons and contrasts. Older children, notably boys, are intrigued by this author's socially powerful tale *The Man*. Waking up, a boy finds a manikin beside him. For three days he has to attend to his every need, keep him a secret, and engage in arguments about their different life-styles, language and cultural assumptions about the world. The book is big enough for a group of readers to stand round it and read the dialogues like a playscript.

The unconventional appearance of the pages and experiments with words and images in depictions of the manikin's ferocity and the boy's confusion, invite a visual–linguistic probing that has no direct counterpart in adult texts. Whatever the print-locked, powerful literates decree about reading in school, artists and illustrators are in the driving seat in children's encounters with books.

Television both supports and challenges those whose work is pictorial. We assume that children don't need lessons to interpret moving images but, in fact, programme-makers organise the perceptions of their audience. With still pictures, readers interpret a sequence of images by means of subtly-directed looking. They operate a kind of radial gaze to follow the different appearances of a central character while, at the same time, taking in the peripheral details. More understanding of how children learn to read and more descriptions of their interactions with these complex texts would be helpful.

Quentin Blake is the doyen of British picture book-makers. Intellectually and creatively he communicates his respect for children's intelligence and imagination. His distinctive style – pen and wash drawings of thin limbed children in expressive poses, gazing directly from eyes no more than dots – is well known. Thousands of children devoted to the stories of Roald Dahl remember Matilda, The Big Friendly Giant, Danny, the Champion of the World and others as Blake depicts them. He has also brought the elusive genius of Russell Hoban closer to readers of *The Rain Door*, *Monsters* and *How Tom Beat Captain Najork and His Hired Sportsmen* and demonstrates the contemporaneity of canonical texts like Belloc's *Algernon and Other Cautionary Tales*. The quirky movements of his characters, Patrick, Simpkin, Mrs Armitage, Professor Dupont and others, are accompanied by words and phrases that children learn to recite with bravura. Mr Magnolia, who had only one boot, lets his creator play with the phonological irregularities of English spelling: *boot* rhymes with *flute*, *newt*, *suit* and *salute*. A book for reception class reading, *All Join In*, shows a group of undisciplined minors creating mayhem, noisily, as they sort out the kitchen pans. The readers are encouraged to join in the noise-making, phonologically.

Picture book artists join with skilled writers to display traditional tales in new guise for each new generation. A recent retelling by Naomi Lewis of Andersen's *The Emperor's New Clothes* combines an impeccable text with sophisticated illustrations by Angela Barrett. The setting is 'a small kingdom', curiously like Monaco, at the end of a *belle epoque*, 1913. The Emperor's real clothes have an authenticity they usually lack, and his obsession with his appearance is implied in the full sartorial details. Just how convincingly the trick was played by the rascally tailors is shown as silhouettes behind lit windows. Part of the story is in newspaper format. The illusion is kept up for the readers as well as the sycophants until the child, a girl this time, blows the gaff.

There is now a general assumption that children's books will represent faithfully the cultural world of childhood, especially with regard to differences of class, race and gender. The complexity of this can be seen in *The Baby's Catalogue*, a book for young children by Janet and Allan Ahlberg modelled on mail-order catalogues. Immaculate, miniature illustrations of families, their samenesses and differences with regard to babies, toys, teas, books, baths and bedtimes, subtly referenced, gently ironic, are immediately recognised, as is the single word on each page. This is a good example of a text with dual reference; adults and children looking at the book together recognise themselves. Like a family photograph album, but more detailed, *Peepo* offers a glimpse of a parent's wartime childhood. The peephole in the page lets the reader focus on the picture to come, then, turned over, selects something on the one just gone. School reading books are gently mocked in a series of Happy Families. Ahlberg joke books provide pupils with riddles to ask and word tricks to play. *Please, Mrs Butler*, a much loved book of poems, expresses both the paradoxes and agonies of English school life in ways that make them tolerable. In these books, the range and dynamics of reading are more than words and sentences.

An important transition stage in children's reading comes when they confidently know how to 'tune' a text so as to catch the nuances of meaning. They also learn that books beget books. Nowhere do these things happen more richly or joyously than in *The Jolly Postman*, or *Other People's Letters* where the nursery-tale characters reappear from *Each Peach Pear Plum*. Even more significantly, in the envelopes which are pages in the actual book, readers find a letter of apology, an invitation, an advertising flyer, a publisher's promotion, a birthday card, a lawyer's caution, exemplifying the social uses of writing that count as literacy. This kind of literary play and pleasure in texts continues in *The Clothes Horse and other Stories*, where common metaphors become characters and events. 'Life savings' are days of early life saved to be enjoyed later; the clothes horse is made of clothes, the night train brings the night, which is then stolen and retrieved. For more experienced readers there are *The Better Brown Stories* where Allan Ahlberg, in post-modernist mode, acknowledges the help of Robert Louis Stevenson, Sir Arthur Conan Doyle, W. Somerset Maugham, Enid Blyton and Raymond Briggs 'without whose work this book could not have been written'. Literary critics expose the influence of early reading on writers whose work is secure as literature. *Finnegans Wake* is 'a new piece of grown-up child's play in which old juvenile games and rhymes get absorbed and rewritten'.[5] Martha Nussbaum discusses fairytales with the experienced students at Yale Law School.[6] Authors who take children's reading seriously, William Mayne, for example, are confident that their readers will tackle 'writerly' texts if given the chance to discover what the writer is up to.

The current profusion of texts for children makes choice difficult in terms of both content and 'level'. Jacqueline Rose claims that the topics which most engage the young are origins, sex and death, a notion which is even more confusing when these topics are in picture books.[7] Babette Cole's treatment of conception (*Mummy Laid an Egg*), health (*Dr Dog*), old age (*Drop Dead*) and divorce (*Two of Everything*) shows how the matter-of-factness of children's enquiries can be joined with their sense of the ridiculous in the solipsistic oddities of adults. Anne Fine's directness makes her books popular with a wide range of readers, especially the 'chapter' books that usually follow the forced march through the reading scheme. In *Bill's New Frock*, *Design a Pram* and *Flour Babies*, she takes a social convention from the cultural code, so as to call into question gender roles and conventions of classroom behaviour. Bill's pink dress has no pockets and he can't play football; pram design is less gender specific than expected; in carrying bags of flour, boys discover the responsibilities of parenthood. The National Curriculum makes frequent reference to 'challenging texts'. Anne Fine represents the great number of gifted writers whose texts teach what children are glad to be challenged to learn.

Boys are presented as a special case. The 1993 report from Ofsted stressed the poor achievement of many boys in secondary schools who, in their early learning lacked 'models of males who invest much time and energy in literacy'. Teachers are now encouraged to 'challenge the roles and expectations boys adopt'.[8] These statements are strange in the light of the prominence of male writers of books for boys and the leading roles played by men in children's literature studies more generally. Aidan Chambers, novelist, critic, teacher, is a case in point. Michael Foreman's autobiographical account of his wartime childhood, *War Boy*, combines the seriousness of actual events, wearing a gas mask, for example, with a young person's views on them. Phillip Pullman has come to the fore as a writer who demonstrates new textualities. The mock-Gothic of *Count Karlstein* or the *Ride of the Huntsman* combines conventions of literature, music and film; *Clockwork*, a variation on the Faust legend, is an 'invention' in the sense used by Bach – two narrators and two stories in counterpoint; two volumes of a trilogy, *His Dark Materials*, is a complex quest tale with strong Miltonic resonances. The potential of modern heroism combined with ancient legend may have been underplayed in many boys' early experiences, where 'sitting there, reading' hasn't met with approval, and reading lessons have lacked enchantment. Ted Hughes' *The Iron Man* is still the best modern myth for a technological age.

To find books that boys will read with interest, choosers generally assume that facts are more important than fantasy. This may be so, but I guess that peer pressure also plays a part. Boys are many among the current readers of poetry, surely one of the success stories of children's reading. The popularity of poets in schools shows that children's involvement goes far beyond phonological awareness. Every verbal trick that works: jokes, riddles, farcical comparisons, the legacy of Carroll and Lear, their modern counterparts and the contents of Ted Hughes and Seamus Heaney's *The School Bag*, all redeem the notion that boys don't read because reading is hard to learn and difficult to sustain. My concern is that the magic of poetry should not be overwhelmed by too many earnest endeavours to make it earn its keep. One thing more: boys are intrigued by subversions. J. Scieszka's *The Stinky Cheeseman and Other Fairly Stupid Tales* entrusts young readers with post-modern aporia – 'Who is this ISBN guy?' 'Where is that lazy author?' – good for showing off what isn't taught in lessons.

The main problem for teachers is that their best and most effective skills in teaching reading are constantly undervalued: observing, interacting, taking children's thinking further, making split-second decisions at significant points of learning and following these up with reflection shared in discussions. To learn to read better than ever before, as they surely must, children need space and time to *think* about what they are reading and also about reading itself. This means that texts of worth, literature especially, must be moved to the centre, to become the core of the reading curriculum. This is not a rejection of confirmed ways of teaching reading. My proposal is about texts, and the difference books make to children's views of the task of learning to read; a simple shift, to bring the writers and artists who care about readers into closer contact with those who have to engage with *new* texts.

This move has already been made, in theory and practice, at the Centre for Language in Primary Education. In *The Core Book*, Sue Ellis, Myra Barrs and their colleagues discuss 'the use of children's books as a central resource within a *structured approach* [my italics] to reading in the primary school, and the key role of children's literature in the reading curriculum to enhance children's progress as readers'. They acknowledge that the actual proposals are not new. Over the past 15 years, many teachers and schools have seen in the texts of modern children's books how authors and illustrators support children's different ways of learning to read and write and extend their view of reading more generally. What is new is a *systematic* use of children's literature in the hands of accomplished teachers (and there are many) to demonstrate all aspects of the reading process. What is different is the provision of core book collections with annotated lists, which distinguish for teachers, at each stage, two central functions: support for children's learning to read, and the provision of literature collections to enhance their understanding and progress. The books are not prescribed texts, but carefully selected, annotated examples which can be added to a school's existing resources or used as preferred alternatives. In addition, *The Core Book* includes demonstrations of the books in use and of class work based on them, together with ways of assessing children's progress and how to keep records so as to provide concrete evidence of children's strengths and weaknesses. The text is illustrated with photographs, and drawings by Quentin Blake.[9]

Those who emphasise the functional nature of literacy, who believe that there is a set of 'basic' competences to be taught and learned according to a single pattern of instruction, will have difficulty with the underlying assumptions of this chapter: that literacy is too important to be taught or to serve as an instrumental commodity; that reading lessons in the early years and thereafter are, as Seamus Heaney says of poetry, 'a working model of inclusive consciousness', brought about by readers' interaction with texts and authors who teach them all that reading involves, the games texts play and, significantly, the skill to interrogate the official texts which affect their lives as citizens. I am persuaded that best practice includes reading with children the texts that they are not yet experienced enough to read for themselves, and that the best evidence of reading progress comes from the observations of good teachers who take time to discuss reading with their pupils and who teach them to write.

Notes

1   *Literacy Task Force, A Reading Revolution: How We Can Teach Every Child To Read Well,* The Preliminary Report of the Literacy Task Force, chaired by Professor Michael Barber. Published for consultation 27 February 1997

2   Opie, I. and P., *The Lore and Language of Schoolchildren* (Oxford: The Clarendon Press, 1959)

3   P. Hollindale, *Signs of Childness in Children's Books* (Stroud: The Thimble Press, 1997)

4   G. Kress., *Before Writing: Rethinking the Paths to Literacy* (London: Routledge, 1997)

5   V. Cunningham, *In the Reading Gaol: Postmodernity, Texts, and History* (Oxford: Blackwell, 1994)

6   M. Nussbaum, *Poetic Justice* (Boston: Beacon Press, 1995)
7   J. Rose, *The Case of Peter Pan or The Impossibility of Children's Fiction* (London: Macmillan, 1984)
8   The Qualifications and Curriculum Authority, *Can Do Better: Raising Boys' Achievement in English* (London: QCA, 1998)
9   S. Ellis and M. Barrs, *The Core Book: A Structured Approach to Using Books Within the Reading Curriculum* (London: Centre for Language in Primary Education, 1996)

Changing literacy in the early years of school
Henrietta Dombey

Lessons learnt at the start
The basics of learning to read and write involve far more than the capacity to recognise and reproduce written words with accuracy and fluency, essential though this competence is. What reading and writing are used for matters. The way in which we first encounter reading and writing in school has a profound effect on what we think literacy is good for.

Some of our early primary classrooms give children a sense of the power of the written word to call up experiences, ideas and feelings and give them a kind of order in words that fascinate and reverberate. In others, reading and writing are meaningful, less because of what is said than as ways to win teachers' and parents' approval. They are a means to an end. In English classrooms these different views of early literacy have competed with each other for many decades. The 'richer' view carries the danger that not enough attention will be given to the more mundane aspects of literacy learning. The more instrumental approach runs the risk of communicating to children a very narrow view of what literacy is about and giving them little incentive to wrestle with it. Most teachers in England have taken a fairly eclectic line, incorporating elements of both conceptions. The more successful promote an active, involved and effective literacy. The less successful present their children with a desultory collection of unconnected activities, eliciting little involvement and low levels of accuracy and fluency.

An unsatisfactory curriculum?
With the publication of *The Cox Report* (DES, 1989), the original National Curriculum for English, primary teachers were largely delighted to find that their fears of a detailed, prescriptive and formalist curriculum were unfounded. Instead, they found a considered and informed document, respective of research into language, literacy and their learning and teaching, and concerned to help children make sense of their inner and outer worlds, through a rich and varied use of written and spoken language. The format gave teachers plenty of scope to plan their teaching to cope with the needs and interests of their particular classes.

This happy situation, where teachers voiced only minor complaints about the curriculum, came sharply to an end with the revision of the English curriculum, set in motion on only the thinnest of pretexts. The revised curriculum steered sharply away from helping children to articulate their thoughts and feelings towards a utilitarian view of English in general and of literacy in particular (DfE, 1995). Literature, of course, is not excluded, but veneration of form is given precedence over consideration and articulation of meaning, and there is little place, if any, for exploring the personal significance of a text for a young reader.

Yet with the lack of preparatory research that is the hallmark of officially-sponsored educational innovation in England, primary schools are now being presented with a new conception – the National Literacy Strategy. This will have a far-reaching effect on the content and phasing of literacy teaching and on the transactions through which it is carried out. If the Chief Inspector of Schools has his way, it will even determine the shape of the impending revision of the National Curriculum in English, due to become operational in 2001.

Despite the fact that it has, as yet, no statutory force, all primary schools are being urged to adopt the strategy. As I write this, all over England primary teachers are nervously ordering sets of picture books and big books, too; planning group activities at word, sentence and text level, and desperately trying to dragoon available adults into the classroom to help out with the Literacy Hour. Many teachers at Key Stage 1 feel distinctly apprehensive about what promises to be a total disruption to the established pattern of their reading teaching, particularly to that cornerstone of so much classroom practice, 'hearing' individual children read from their reading scheme books. And there are nagging concerns about the 'cascade' arrangements for the in-service training, which will involve most class teachers in receiving a brief initiation from colleagues (themselves, only briefly initiated) perilously close to the start of the autumn term.

But anxiety seems to be mixed with excitement: teachers who have been working with big books in whole-class sessions and sets of picture books in small group shared-reading sessions see the Literacy Hour as providing a justification and an elaboration of their past efforts – with the bonus of increased resources. Many are delighted that texts of real literary quality are implied by the 'lit crit' activities in the Literacy Framework – the long and detailed document which lays down the content and structure of the Literacy Hour (Standards and Effectiveness Unit, 1998). Many welcome the three-strand approach of attention to word, sentence and text as signalling with useful clarity that learning to read and write are not just matters of word recognition and spelling.

Others are alarmed by the Framework's apparent rigidity – by its presentation of these three levels as operating independently, by the precise timing of group and class work and by the closely prescribed term-by-term specification of content, down to the particular phonemes to be dealt with in any given term. There is concern that daily reading aloud to the class, a practice which initiates children into the delights of the written word through hearing texts more complex than they can read themselves, may be put at risk, as it has no place in the Literacy Hour and schools may be reluctant to find space for it elsewhere. Reception teachers are particularly concerned about very young children, many of whom will be just four at the start of the school year in September, being expected to work within such a constraining framework for an hour at a time every day. Where has it all come from?

Where the National Literacy Strategy has come from
New Labour's National Literacy Strategy contains more than the Literacy Hour, and spreads far beyond schools. It involves parents, community organisations, television companies, BT, supermarkets and many other corporate bodies in spreading the message that reading and writing are important, interesting and achievable. But at its heart is the National Literacy Framework to which, despite an absence of any statutory force, all primary schools are expected to conform from September 1998.

The plans for the Strategy and the Framework, hatched well before the election in May 1997, are a takeover and expansion of an initiative of the previous government, confusingly called the National Literacy Project. The Literacy Framework was originally developed as the centrepiece of this project, the aim of which was to raise the standards of literacy teaching in some 250 of England's lowest-performing primary schools in some 20 authorities. Although a number of educators queried the content and approach of the project, few questioned the need for such an initiative. In tests of primary literacy we, in England, are distinguished from our European partners by our 'long tail of underachievement' (Brooks et al., 1996). Our mid and high achievers can stand comparison with their European equivalents, but we have far too many low achievers, lagging far too far behind their age-mates.

Without waiting for the results of an evaluative study of the project's effectiveness (still not forthcoming at the time of writing), New Labour announced in February 1997 its plans for expanding this project to all schools. The National Literacy Strategy was to be the means by which teachers would achieve Labour's ambitious target for raising the reading and writing scores of 11-year-olds, so that by 2002, 80 per cent should achieve Level 4 in the National Curriculum Literacy tests and by 2007, this should be 95 per cent. 'Level 4' represents what the constructors of the National Curriculum took to be the mean level of what is achievable by this age group, so requiring 95 per cent to achieve it is an inflation of expectation of a very high order.

Despite evidence that there is no clear connection between them (Robinson, 1998), it seems that higher scores on literacy and numeracy for the country's 11-year-olds are expected to reverse the tide of economic decline, unemployment and national uncertainty. Political reputations are staked on achieving these literacy targets, in the hope of achieving larger political ends. So Key Stage 1 teachers are being pressed into service to prepare the ground for their colleagues at Key Stage 2, and the eyes of both are to be firmly fixed on the end of Key Stage tests.

The literacy framework

The Literacy Framework, with its term-by-term specification of what is to be taught at word, sentence and text level, in lists up to 22 items long (27, at Key Stage 2), is a bold pedagogic statement. In a notoriously complex area of learning it is advanced as the one right way to teach, the way that is supported by research and inspection evidence. Yet no specific references support this claim.

But a number of its features seem positive. Certainly research indicates the value of whole-class and group approaches (the Framework's stock in trade) and nothing convincing to support reliance on one-to-one encounters, which many teachers still use as the main vehicle for literacy teaching.

Certainly, there is evidence that powerful literary texts have more lessons to teach than those whose subject matter is more trivial and whose language is more superficial (Meek, 1988). But much of this potential is unrealised in the Framework. Meanwhile the focus and relentless detail of the bottom-up approach to phonics, where children 'build up words' from their constituent phonemes, conflict with much recent research in this area (Bussis et al., 1985; Goswami and Bryant, 1990; Moustafa, 1997). And there is nothing to support the concern, which becomes almost obsessive at Key Stage 2, with the identification of word classes as a route to literacy. No justification is given for the absence of any mention of how, when or even whether the children's progress is to be assessed; one can only assume that assessment carries the danger of showing that not all children profit from this sort of lock-step approach. Nor is there any research evidence to justify either the notion of a daily Literacy Hour, or the subdivision of this hour into prescribed time-slots for whole-class attention to texts, sentences and words, for group work and for sharing the fruits of this with the class.

This does not mean that these features all lack merit: while the absence of assessment is clearly worrying, some features have an inherent attraction and plausibility and are worthy of trialling and development. But should they be put together in a package and presented as the one approved way to teach? This is a pedagogy of untried uniformity. The uniformity denies children's widely varying out-of-school experiences. While the central function of education is to introduce learners to new experience, knowledge and understanding, this is most substantially achieved, particularly where young literacy learners are concerned, if the pedagogy involved is based on some recognition of what the learners already know and have experienced. This means, in part, recognising that children who come to school with vastly different out-of-school experiences of literacy may have rather different needs, leaving some confused and others bored during lengthy whole-class sessions. It also means recognising the value of 'life to text' connections through which children can invest texts with personal significance, and their own lives with enhanced meaning. This is an essential element of literacy learning at all ages. But there is very little room for it in the Literacy Framework.

Nor is there any recognition that the literacy practices of the late twentieth century are changing in important ways. The increasing role of visual images, in newspapers and reports as well as the moving images of film, television and video, are not recognised as meriting attention. Yet children need to learn to interrogate images if they are to read them in an informed and critical way. Hypertext, too, is ignored, although the non-linear nature of such text implies ways of reading that are fundamentally different from the linear reading of narrative text. Some very young children are encountering such texts at home, and learning to navigate their individual routes through complex webs of information. But an introduction in the classroom to the possibilities of these new ways of reading finds no place in the Literacy Framework, which shows no concern to prepare children for the literacies of the twenty-first century.

Instead the focus is on an arid formalism more appropriate to the nineteenth century. Children are to be taught 'to note key structural features in a text' (Year 2, Term 1) and such bizarre practices as 'to turn statements into questions, learning a range of "wh" words' (Year 2, Term 3). They are to be apprised of (some of) the rules that govern language, but not invited to engage in activities which give it real shape, purpose and significance.

For all its explicitness about procedures, the Literacy Framework is curiously reticent about the purposes of literacy teaching and learning. 'Literacy' we are told 'unites the important skills of reading and writing' (Standards and Effectiveness Unit, 1998, p. 3). Mention is made, at the end of a long list of technical competences, of enjoyment, evaluation, justification of preferences, imagination, inventiveness and critical awareness. But these appear, like a little-used list of desserts, detached from the menu that precedes them – to be enjoyed if at all only after pupils have eaten up all their nutritious technical cabbage. They are unlikely to flourish from strict application of the Framework.

There is no sense of the rich texture of classrooms where literacy learning is urgent and purposeful; no sense of the vital part that literacy can play in the social and emotional lives of young children; no sense of the lessons learned through the imaginative exploration of painful experiences in the company of gifted authors and artists; no sense that writing about an experience can help a child to order it and come to terms with it – can 'help you sort things out in your mind' in the words of a troubled 7-year-old; no sense of reading and writing put to work, enabling children to encounter other times, places and points of view – rather than remaining imprisoned in the here and now.

Of course techniques matter; without them nothing substantial can be achieved. But unless children experience the richer meanings that literacy can give them, they are unlikely to become literate in the sense of making their own active use of literacy outside school as well as in.

Teaching transactions

As to the transactions through which this curriculum is to be taught, despite protestations, these are essentially didactic. 'Interaction' should not be taken to mean hospitality to children's ideas. A teacher should not allow herself to deviate from the clearly stated intentions of what she wishes a group of children to learn in a particular session. If the teacher's focus is on sentence structure, the children should not be allowed to deviate from this, no matter if a child makes a challenging observation on the text under discussion, perhaps raising issues of morality or word patterns. All of this runs quite counter to Wells' research on productive teaching sessions in Toronto classrooms, and to the characteristics of successful literacy teaching which Cambourne finds to operate in Australian classrooms (Wells, 1992; Cambourne, 1997).

Wells finds, as in all language learning, negotiation to be the key feature of productive practice in literacy learning. While the teacher clearly needs a carefully thought-out agenda, this should not preclude recognition of and response to children's concerns and queries. Indeed, openness to these may be an important contributor to raising children's involvement in their learning and expectations of themselves. Cambourne finds that successful literacy teaching practices 'coerce learners to draw on more than one sub-system of language', involving, for example, both phonics and larger text meanings. And as well as being explicit and systematic, successful literacy teaching practices are also contextualised in the rich to and fro of class-room life, and mindful, in that they invite reflection.

For better or worse?
Stimulated by *The Cox Report* and agencies such as the Centre for Language in Primary Education, the last decade has seen a movement towards these more 'mindful' approaches to literacy teaching and learning in our primary schools. Publications such as *The Core Book* (Ellis and Barrs, 1996) have both reflected and shaped the development of thoughtful class and group approaches to central texts, involving reflective reading, exploratory discussion and sustained writing on significant themes. Such progress is put at serious risk by the Literacy Framework, which reduces group reading to 20-minute sessions, advocates clear control of discussion and insists on a focus on technique in all writing tasks. The imposition of this universal solution to all schools' literacy problems is likely to hamper the progress of many children, particularly the very youngest, the bilingual, the more able and the more thoughtful.

But, nonetheless, many primary heads and classroom teachers have welcomed the Framework, especially those who are not English specialists. Many feel a burden has been removed, a set of secrets shared, allowing teachers to get on with the job of teaching while reducing the time spent on planning. They welcome a common approach to a daily literacy hour and the detailed specification of content. But, in the next breath, they express a fervent hope that flexibility will be permitted; that 15-minute sessions might sometimes be read as 10 or 20; that one big book session might include attention at both text and word level; that the phonics teaching might be framed in a more whole to part approach; that the system might be adapted to cater for the needs of children with literacy difficulties and children for whom English is an additional language, and that the whole procedure should be interpreted very loosely in Reception.

This would be a very English response to the very un-English threat of totalitarianism in the classroom. And, up to a point, it might work, provided that schools are well supplied with alluring and challenging texts, and provided that they approach all the teaching sessions in a more interactive spirit than that which imbues the Literacy Framework. Certainly it will enable many teachers to feel more comfortable with the Strategy.

But any kind of adherence to this Framework will have a corrosive influence on the more reflective acts of reading and writing – whether collaborative or individual. If children need a literacy which opens their minds and enlarges their sympathies as well as their understanding, they need teachers who know what literacy can do for them; who have developed a coherent and imaginative approach to their teaching and who know that teaching is an interactive enterprise in which assessment of children's difficulties, competences and interests has a central importance. A framework that imposes literacy teaching by numbers may help some teachers push their pupils through the hoops of the Standard Assessment Tests (SATS), but it will not help them meet the complex literacy needs of the next century.

References

Brooks, G., Pugh, A. K. and Schagen, I. (1996), *Reading Performance at Nine* (Slough: National Foundation for Educational Research)

Bussis, A., Chittenden, E., Amarel, M. and Klausner, E. (1985), *Inquiry into Meaning: An Investigation of Learning to Read* (Hillsdale, NJ: Lawrence Erlbaum Associates)

Cambourne, B. (1997), 'Becoming literate: routes and choices'. Plenary presentation at annual UKRA conference in Manchester

DES, (1989), *English for Ages 5 to 16* (London: HMSO)

DfEE, (1995), *English in the National Curriculum* (London: HMSO)

Ellis, S. and Barrs, M. (1996), *The Core Book: A Structured Approach to Using Books Within the Reading Curriculum* (London: Centre for Language in Primary Education)

Goswami, U. and Bryant, P. (1990), *Phonological Skills and Learning to Read* (Norwood, NJ: Lawrence Erlbaum Associates)

Literacy Task Force (1997), *The Implementation of the National Literacy Strategy* (London: DfE)

Meek, Margaret (1988), *How Texts Teach What Readers Learn* (Stroud, Glos.: The Thimble Press)

Moustafa, M. (1997), *Beyond Traditional Phonics: Research Discoveries and Reading Instruction* (Portsmouth, NH: Heinemann)

O'Sullivan, O. (ed.) (1995), *The Primary Language Record in Use* (London: Centre for Language in Primary Education)

Robinson, P. (1998), 'The tyranny of league tables: international comparisons of educational attainment and economic performance'. Paper prepared for a seminar on Comparative Research on Pupil Achievement, University of Bristol, 3 March 1998

Standards and Effectiveness Unit (1998), *The National Literacy Strategy: Framework for Teaching* (London: DfEE)

Wells, C.G. (1992), *Constructing Knowledge Together – Classrooms as Centers of Inquiry and Literacy,* (Portsmouth, NH: Heinemann/Cassell)

Reading in the primary school
Terry Furlong

Typically, there are three strands to the development of children's reading experience as organised by successful teachers. With the youngest children, teachers often present a 'big book', say *Mr Gumpy's Outing*, to the whole class, then read it and discuss it with them, building other work out of the book and what the children had been interested in, over the next couple of weeks. With older children, the teacher might be reading a short novel like *Carrie's War* or *The Iron Man*. Without detracting from the children's pleasure or their enjoyment of the story, teachers use the books to teach children quite a lot about words and the letters which make them; about punctuation and word order; in fact, all kinds of things about the writing system and the ways in which it works. This is all quite seamlessly mixed with proper concerns about what would happen next, why things happened, why people behaved in the way they did, and all the aspects of plot, setting, characterisation and authorship which make stories so interesting and enjoyable. These colleagues also use non-fiction texts in similar ways for different purposes.

A second strand involves pupils reading for themselves – from nursery children 'behaving like readers' to Year 5 and Year 6 pupils choosing their own fiction and non-fiction to read. A whole host of strategies is used to encourage, develop and maintain individual reading for interest and pleasure: class libraries, school libraries, public libraries, book clubs, book weeks, bookmaking and writing, illustrating, individual reading assignments, 'public' readings, tape recording, book recommending and reviewing, and so on. The important thing is to create a school culture in which reading has a high profile and in which all children *and their teachers* are involved in developing their own tastes and interests in reading.

The third strand involves reading with others. In the earliest years, this often formalised in a system of parents and children reading together. As soon as children begin to pick up the first signs of independence in reading, they are encouraged to read to each other, or to tell/read their own stories on to tape, and this leads on to various kinds of paired and small group reading activities which become regular features of these junior classrooms.

I have not, in this brief snapshot, mentioned published reading schemes. This is because they can play a limited role in only the second of these strands; they can be used to help pupils' development as individual readers, as part of a much wider picture of individual development, but, even here, many teachers would feel that once children have become fairly confident independent readers, reading schemes are no longer so useful, whatever their publishers may claim. What schemes cannot do is the essential work that the teacher does in what I have called the first strand of development.

There the teacher 'models' reading for the children, not just in the sense of how to read aloud effectively and interestingly, but by making explicit, through class discussion, all the kinds of questions readers have to have in their heads if they are to enter into a dialogue with the author. It is here, too, that the teacher shows children what understanding and real comprehension are all about: comparing the ideas, experiences, understandings, knowledge and information that children meet in the text with their own. That is, after all, why reading is useful and entertaining, and it is what real learning is all about. Just as a good art teacher teaches children how to 'look with intent', so a real reading teacher teaches children how to 'engage with' a text. Nobody else, other than a teacher with a roomful of children, is in a position to do this.

Just as vital is the third strand of development where children can share their likes and dislikes, their understandings and confusions, their enthusiasms and their questions with others of their own age and experience. Here they can ask questions they would not ask in front of the teacher and the whole class, make connections and compare views at a personal level, without in any way being held to account for them. They can have several goes at trying to understand something or make themselves clear without others getting bored and the teacher feeling that things need to move on. In this context, they learn such things as how to find their way back into a story; they learn to locate specific information, to develop notions like relevance and to deal with really challenging questions. One only has to see a Year 6 'poor reader' working with a much younger pupil to understand how much more successfully we can learn when we are involved in trying to teach someone else than when we are being taught ourselves.

When I became an adviser and inspector of schools I had plenty of opportunity to see how wonderfully well this kind of approach worked when it was developed throughout the whole age range from 4 to 12-year-olds: it worked well for the brightest and most experienced readers, recently arrived learners of English as a second or third language, children who needed considerable additional support with literacy, and all kinds of children in between. What impressed me most was that in schools which worked in these kinds of ways, children continued to develop as readers throughout the junior years, irrespective of the character of the local area and the social needs of the children. Of course, some children read more than others and could be said to have developed their skills as readers to a higher level than others, but teachers in these schools very rarely spoke of 'reluctant readers' or 'non-readers'.

Such schools became, if you like, my benchmark for the successful teaching of reading. By any measure one cared to choose, from reading with pupils and talking to them to standardised tests of various sub-skills of reading, virtually all the pupils were reasonable or very successful readers. Even those pupils who had statements specifying their difficulties with language and the acquisition of literacy, made fairly continuous, if not startling, progress. The kind of child who was genuinely rare in these schools and their classes, but all too common in many other schools, was the 'plateau' child: a child who is more or less an independent reader, who can 'decode' print at a straightforward level and might register on a standardised test with a 'reading age' of about 8 or 9 years. Typically, these are children who have made reasonable progress throughout their infant years, but who lose confidence and/or interest at some point during the junior years.

One is bound to ask why, in some schools, there are so many more children who stop making progress in reading, or at least whose rate of progress slows very considerably. Not so very long ago, I was in a junior classroom which was so bare that the most interesting things in it, apart from the children, were a broken cupboard door and a baseball bat. In the children's 'Language' books, there was nothing except dictation exercises and the attempted answers to dire 'comprehension' material, republished in 1964. Exceptional, you might reasonably say. Outrageous, after six or seven years of a National Curriculum for English.

I do know other schools where the reading for junior-aged pupils is quite inadequate. Reading consists for the most part of the following elements: sustained silent reading, or pretending to for some pupils, for 15 to 20 minutes daily; comprehension exercises on a mixture of extracts; and class discussion of teacher-chosen pieces of material for science, humanities or other curriculum areas. There may be occasional additions of better practice for at least some of the pupils, like small group reading for those judged competent readers. And there is often fairly heavy reliance on some 'English' workbook or other. The whole experience of reading is 'bitty' and lacks coherence. Beyond a Special Educational Needs Co-ordinator, or an occasional teaching assistant, there is little consistent help given to those who are really struggling and there is little genuine monitoring of children's progress other than an occasional test.

I do not have to believe every utterance from Ofsted to recognise some truth in the following from the most recent annual report: 'The lack in many schools of a structured programme of reading for Key Stage 2 pupils is unacceptable. Greater attention must be given to the range and progression of reading materials to make sure that pupils who have gained good reading skills and an appetite for reading by the end of Key Stage 1 extend and improve their reading sufficiently throughout Key Stage 2' (Standards and Quality in Education 1996/97, Ofsted, February 1998). Only the very suspicious would read this as a plea to provide reading scheme materials throughout the key stage. Range, in National Curriculum terms, is not something which even the better schemes would claim to provide, which is not to say they may not still have a minor role to play, especially with less experienced pupils.

The key phrases for me in the chief inspector's report are 'range and progression', 'good reading skills' and 'an appetite for reading'. Both versions of the National Curriculum have been quite clear about the wide range of reading material pupils need to have experienced, first-hand, and the post-Dearing version was much more prescriptive about it than the original devised by Professor's Cox's Committee. The recently published *Framework for Teaching* by the National Literacy Project is in many ways even more instrumental and prescriptive, but it is quite specific about the range of reading required. It ought to be perfectly clear, by now, that what I have called the second strand of the reading curriculum cannot guarantee this range. Only the teachers can plan this through a mixture of texts read to and with the whole class and by organising appropriate reading for small groups within the class. Individually chosen, or guided, reading can supplement, extend or deepen this range, but it cannot easily provide it. As to reading skills, texts may be able to teach children many things, as Margaret Meek made clear, but they cannot be expected to do everything for all children. Children vary greatly in the degree of explicit knowledge which they need in order to be able to develop existing skills as readers further, or to acquire new ones. The 'good reading skills' which the report talks about are presumably those listed in the 'skills' section of the National Curriculum for English. Year 3 pupils will have gained them from a mixture of sources: the variety of texts they can read for themselves, their own experience, errors and successes, other children in their class, and their teacher who can show, explain and answer questions for them. It helps enormously if a certain amount of that experience arises from common texts which are shared by the pupils and the teacher, and the discussion of strategies, skills and understanding has become a commonplace of classroom experience. There are now more useful materials published which support this common experience, like the Shared Reading booklets published by the National Association for the Teaching of English (NATE) and others. The lonely furrow of the scheme book, or even sustained silent reading, tends to give most to those who already have and know how to get more.

The third section of the current National Curriculum for English, 'Standard English and language study' is more controversial, but not in relation to reading, where its requirements are brief and sensible. The recent *Framework for Teaching* document from the National Literacy Project, however, where the requirements for reading and writing are combined, is a different matter. The 'text level' work requirements are extremely demanding.

How demanding? How about: 'discuss the merits and limitations of instructional texts, including IT and other media texts'; or 'compare forms and types of humour'? Both of these are taken from the requirements for Year 3 pupils (8-and 9-year olds). There is nothing like this in the current National Curriculum requirements for Key Stage 2, or even for that matter at Key Stages 3 and 4. Many undergraduate students would find these challenging. Such is the degree of mismatch between the National Curriculum in English and the requirements of the National Literacy Strategy that we risk damaging confusion.

In addition to the work at the level of the whole text, the Teaching Framework specifies in extraordinary detail the work which children are supposed to do at the level of the sentence and the individual word. Much refers specifically to writing, like spelling and handwriting, but a great deal else is expected to be learned through the detailed examination of reading materials. For example, junior age children are expected to acquire considerable knowledge of the grammatical functions of words and a secure understanding of clausal relationships in complex and compound sentences which very few O Level candidates ever exhibited.

There is a clear danger that, in some classrooms, the important pleasures and understandings which gradually evolve through the experience of reading could be lost if the 'penalty' for reading together is too much close textual analysis. It takes great skill and sensitivity by teachers to achieve an acceptable balance between the macro- and micro-features of particular texts and this varies as between novels, stories, poems, drama and the various kinds of non-fiction texts. There is also a danger that the number of detailed requirements for explicit knowledge and understanding at the level of word and sentence might mislead some teachers into a curriculum dominated by short scope 'exercises', 'practice' and very instrumental teaching. The whole document seems to assume, on no declared evidence, that children of these ages will be capable of understanding, retaining and using this explicit knowledge.

Perhaps I am worrying unnecessarily: good teachers will sort out the confusions, concentrate on the useful and possible, and ignore the useless and impossible, as they always do. But my concern is for the children referred to in the Chief Inspector's report – those who may have 'gained an appetite for reading' but who fail to develop further, or worse, lose that appetite altogether, as far too many, especially boys, do.

It is for them that the reading curriculum needs to be improved and it is their interest and motivation which needs to be increased. Yet where in the instrumental and hectoring language of these official documents does anyone speak about children's motivation to read; about how teachers get them interested in new topics, new authors and new forms of written language? Whatever happened to the language of the original national curriculum requirements for reading, such as: 'Reading should be promoted as an enjoyable activity ... Pupils should develop as enthusiastic and reflective readers ... They should be reading extensively for their own interest ... Opportunities for reading should include independent reading and the study of books by groups and the whole class'? (Taken from the stage-related programme of study (Key Stage 2), *English for Ages 5–16*, HMSO, 1993.)

What happens in the effective schools described earlier in this essay is that through the three strands of reading experience, teachers create an atmosphere in which reading, and an enthusiasm for it, is the norm. These teachers know that children learn quickest when they are *really* interested, so they spend time discovering individual children's interests and finding things which particular pupils might like to read – fiction and non-fiction. They create the right balance between introducing new and often important texts to the whole class or groups and the monitoring and development of individual readers. Their head teachers do not allow the recurrent financial crises to deplete the flow of new and interesting books coming into classrooms and libraries. Most importantly, these schools understand that motivating pupils is vital and do everything they can to foster and encourage it. They also know that there are no quick fixes, that no instrumental recipe from publishing houses, government quangos or even CD-ROMs can substitute for the pupil's experience as a more and more successful reader; that although readers at all stages of development will have much more in common, there is much that is particular to individual students.

We would all like to extend this enjoyable and successful experience of reading to those junior age children who get far less of it than they deserve. Even those who believe that this can be done by coercion and instruction, sorry 'pressure', whether of children or their teachers, would agree. But how would we know whether this had happened or not? How do we measure progress in reading at Key Stage 2? Each school has its own preferred methods for assessing progress, of course, but nationally we have only two instruments – inspection and national tests. Inspection, though to some degree impressionistic, can give us a feel for the broader picture and for the amount and quality of reading experience. It can also tell us in broad terms, by talking with pupils and reading their written work, some things about the rates at which students are making progress, or not.

However, the government and the nation seems to have committed itself to the end of the Key Stage 2 test as some kind of litmus paper by which success and progress in reading will be measured. Teachers' own assessments of pupils' progress against the full range of criteria set out in the 'level descriptions' are supposed to be reported alongside the results of the tests, and are supposed to be accorded equal status. Since virtually no time or support is given to schools to moderate these assessments within their own institutions and there is no mechanism to allow comparison or interpretation of standards between schools, locally, regionally or nationally, this is becoming something of an irritating joke. Important users of the information like Ofsted, government quangos and secondary schools, blatantly ignore them, and no one has thought fit to consult the students or their parents about what they think. That leaves us with the national test.

So what is this test and what does it tell us about pupils' progress in the National Curriculum for reading? The test asks students to read a story (in 1997, about three sides of A4 paper in largish type) and then to read some information texts (again about three sides in 1997). Students have 15 minutes to read this material and then 45 minutes to answer about 30 mainly comprehension-type questions about the passages (in 1997, 19 on the story and 10 on the non-fiction texts) for 50 marks. Let me say straightaway that the tests have improved over the three years they have been running (1995, 1996 and 1997): the texts have become of a more manageable length and have become better 'pitched'; the wording of questions has become clearer and less ambiguous; the marking guidance less tendentious, and so on. I am even prepared to believe that the marking is now less inaccurate and more consistent than it has been in past years.

Even so, it is a very narrow measure of reading that suffers from many of the usual weaknesses of comprehension exercises, and this kind of timed test, in particular: multiple choice questions, information fishing, word and phrase identification, questions phrased in the negative, looking for preconceived answers, and so on. Questions for multiple marks, asking for views, opinions, deduction or interpretation, give little indication of the complexity of answers expected for the three marks beyond 'explain as fully as you can', and often not even that. The best that can be said of it is that it attempts to sample, very briefly and very narrowly, some of the things that children of this age are expected to be able to do as a result of having followed the National Curriculum for reading. The 'range' demanded by the programme of study is reduced to what I have described: the 'skills' are restricted to those very few which can be tested on this type of material in this context. Only in a very loose way can the marks gained out of 50 be related to the level descriptions given in the statutory curriculum.

In broad terms, it may give some picture of what children in general can do in this type of test: that it over-rewards some and does serious injustice to others is a minor concern. All headline writers, and governments it seems, are concerned with is the percentage of youngsters who didn't reach whatever mark is designated at the cut-off point for the 'award' of a Level 4 or more – the expected standard. (The curriculum was designed with Level 4 as the *average* standard.) That the test was actually very different in all three years and in no way comparable is conveniently ignored. 'Standards are improving – we should be encouraged'. Well, up to a point.

What disturbs me is the influence this test is having upon what is taught to Year 6 children – the reading curriculum. Like all comprehension tests, the pattern of question-setting and expected response is limited and predictable. The longer it continues, the better teachers get at preparing their pupils to perform this particular series of tricks on demand. If this is what the National Curriculum requires reading to be, it is scarcely surprising that in some schools the reading curriculum is mistakenly narrowed to practice at comprehension exercises. It is, after all, hallowed by tradition and regularly cashed in on by some publishing houses. This kind of exercise has been used to test reading since the days of the 11+ examinations. So that's all right then, isn't it?

So, to conclude, have the three versions of the National Curriculum in English (one every three years) helped to improve the reading experience of junior age children, in terms of more pupils becoming confident and competent readers, developing their own tastes and interests and able to deal with a wide range of material? The answer, unfortunately, is that nobody really knows. Secondary head teachers have expressed open disbelief in the levels awarded by Key Stage 2 tests; evidence from other sources like Ofsted is patchy. There are certainly some schools where the pressure to fit in the National Curriculum in other subjects squeezed time devoted to reading very hard: little except extracts, comprehension and silent reading survived in some places, hence the Literacy Hour and the Secretary of

State's insistence that time be found for it. Will the National Literacy Strategy help? The designated hour might, and extra books are a step in the right direction, but unless teachers are able to strike the right balance between word, sentence and whole text, it doesn't look promising. And how will we know if we've got there? Ask me another, preferably multiple choice. I like choices, *when* they're available.

References

DES (1989), *English for Ages 5–16* (London: HMSO)

DFE (1993), *English for Ages 5–16* (London: HMSO)

DfE (1995), *The National Curriculum (England)* (London: HMSO)

DfEE (1998), *The National Literacy Strategy: Framework for Teaching*

SCAA (now QCA) (1995, 1996, 1997), *Reading Booklet for KS2 English Test*

SCAA (now QCA) (1995, 1996, 1997), *Reading Answer Booklet for KS2 English Test*

SCAA (now QCA) (1995, 1996, 1997), *English Test Mark Schemes for KS2*

Meek, M. (1988), *How Texts Teach What Readers Learn* (Exeter: Thimble Press)

NATE (1997) (ed. Bob Bibby) *NATE Shared Reading – Journey to Jo'burg, Carrie's War, The Iron Man, Tom's Midnight Garden* (Sheffield: NATE)

Reading for pupils aged 11 to 14
John Wilks

In 1993, the Conservative government introduced a completely revised English National Curriculum not in tune with the viewpoints of the vast majority of teachers of English. The assessment arrangements at Key Stage 3 (14-year-olds) were equally unacceptable and led, in 1993, to a boycott of the tests by teachers. This division between government diktat and good practice in the schools continues to the present day. It is to be hoped that during the National Year of Reading the Labour government will consult the profession and take into account the considerable amount of research on how to encourage reading among pupils aged 11 to 14.

There are three interrelated issues that need to be addressed to assist teachers to enable significant progress in reading to be made by the nation's young teenagers: the centrally defined and prescribed national reading curriculum; the way in which reading is assessed; and the lack of support for work on electronic media texts. In the first years at secondary school many pupils, including some of the most able, abandon reading for pleasure. Most teachers of English agree that the present curriculum and assessment procedures hinder them in their efforts to cope with this problem.

Prescription in the National Curriculum
The literary canon as defined in the National Curriculum feels more like a threat than an opportunity to English teachers. Although 'range' of texts is often mentioned, there is an unwelcome degree of prescription with a strong bias towards the traditional. The requirements for Key Stages 3 and 4 (secondary school pupils) read as follows:

In the course of Key Stages 3 and 4, pupils reading should include:
- two plays by Shakespeare;
- drama by major playwrights, e.g. Christopher Marlowe, J. B. Priestley, George Bernard Shaw, R. B. Sheridan;
- two works of fiction of high quality by major writers, published before 1900, drawn from those by Jane Austen, Charlotte Brontë, Emily Brontë, John Bunyan, Wilkie Collins, Arthur Conan Doyle, Daniel Defoe, Charles Dickens, George Eliot, Henry Fielding, Elizabeth Gaskell, Thomas Hardy, Henry James, Mary Shelley, Robert Louis Stevenson, Jonathan Swift, Anthony Trollope, H. G. Wells;
- two works of fiction of high quality by major writers with well-established critical reputations, whose works were published after 1900, e.g. William Golding, Graham Greene, James Joyce, D. H. Lawrence, Muriel Spark;

- poems of high quality by four major poets, whose works were published before 1900 drawn from those by Matthew Arnold, Elizabeth Barrett Browning, William Blake, Emily Brontë, Robert Browning, Robert Burns, Lord Byron, Geoffrey Chaucer, John Clare, Samuel Taylor Coleridge, John Donne, John Dryden, Thomas Gray, George Herbert, Robert Herrick, Gerard Manley Hopkins, John Keats, Andrew Marvell, John Milton, Alexander Pope, Christina Rossetti, Shakespeare (sonnets), Percy Bysshe Shelley, Edmund Spenser, Alfred Lord Tennyson, Henry Vaughan, William Wordsworth, Sir Thomas Wyatt;
- poems of high quality by four major poets with well-established critical reputations, whose works were published after 1900, e.g. T. S. Eliot, Thomas Hardy, Seamus Heaney, Ted Hughes, Philip Larkin, R. S. Thomas, W. B. Yeats.

We have, thankfully, abandoned the infamous anthology introduced by John Patten in 1992, when he was Secretary of State for Education. This was a collection of extracts which reflected nostalgia for a lost golden age of pastoral bliss: 'A Child's Christmas in Wales', 'Home Thoughts from Abroad', 'Adlestrop', 'Daffodils'. The mood was so determinedly retrospective that even the youngest living writer (date of birth, 1944) was represented by a poem entitled 'Yesterday'. The selection would have been thought tedious by almost all pupils.

In the latest prescriptions, however, the over-emphasis on the English literary heritage continues, especially when this is reinforced by the criticisms of Ofsted inspectors. This does not provide a reading curriculum to suit all pupils in all regions from all classes and from all cultural backgrounds. It is amazing that the list includes no Commonwealth writers. Why?

Although there have been attempts to justify the reading curriculum by describing it as an 'entitlement curriculum', it is clear that pupils are entitled only to the curriculum chosen for them by politicians and bureaucrats nostalgic for their own schooldays. 'Read what you're given' is the order of the day. At times it feels as if to be an English teacher is to be a collaborator in the imposition of an alien culture which is excluding pupils, sometimes physically. As an experienced teacher, author and editor pointed out in the *TES* recently: 'The fundamental goal of many teachers and of the National Curriculum itself – to promote reading for pleasure beyond mainstream texts – seems increasingly precarious' (Geoff Barton, *TES*, 27 February 1998).

The most exciting new writing in English during the last 30 years or so has often come from non-English backgrounds: Toni Morrison, Michael Ondaatje, Margaret Atwood, Grace Nichols, Salman Rushdie, Timothy Mo,

Kazuo Ishiguro, Alice Walker, Maya Angelou. In the 1980s *The Color Purple* was possibly the most popular book among London's teenagers. Teachers need freedom to introduce their pupils to writings which they think will attract their enthusiasm. When pupils find an author they like they should be encouraged to continue with other works by the same writer, rather than forced to turn aside to a prescribed list of set books.

Teachers need to use their professional skills to make connections between the popular and the unfamiliar, between the concrete and the abstract. We need first, however, to be allowed to construct a reading curriculum that reflects teachers' knowledge and enthusiasm, that builds on pupils' needs and interests before then leading on to increasingly unfamiliar and demanding texts. Pupils need to be shown how to construct themselves as readers. Boys, particularly, need to be encouraged to discuss and reflect on their reading skills and habits and then to set themselves ambitious targets for broadening their reading horizons. They do not need to be in the firing line of a reading curriculum defined by Government diktat. A narrowly prescribed curriculum will lead many of them to stop reading for pleasure. Encouraging a love of reading would be easier if the assessment regime at Key Stage 3 wasn't so intrusive ...

Testing, testing

Central Government has been able to determine which texts are read and how they should be read through controlling the assessment arrangements.

1. The 75-minute Shakespeare test

The following extract from a long discursive essay about *Macbeth* was *not* written in a Key Stage 3 test:

> *If I was directing this play I would set it in a modern day environment. The witches would be tramps and their 'cave' would be a subway. They would live in huts made out of rubbish. I think this would work because many people are fearful and disgusted by tramps. In Act 4 Scene 1 Macbeth enters the subway to find the witches. They taunt Macbeth deeper and deeper into the underground tunnels below London. The apparitions are people who live down there.*
>
> *The tunnels and darkness symbolise him being trapped in his own now dark and twisted mind, not able to turn back. And as he moves further and further into the tunnels it becomes harder and harder to turn back. Instead of thunder there would be the sound of hammering on rails, like criminals rattling the bars of their cell.*

This writing by a Year 10 boy (age 14) was done for GCSE coursework. It shows a real engagement with the play, an understanding of the significance of the witches and an awareness of the cultural context within which an audience interprets the play. It is very unlikely that anything like it would be produced for the 75-minute Key Stage 3 Shakespeare test, partly because of the time constraint but mainly because of the approach to reading embodied in these tests. The emphasis is on understanding passages rather than personal response.

English teachers want pupils to enjoy Shakespeare and know that pupils' enthusiasm for Shakespeare can easily be curtailed by a tedious focus on the set scene. It is ridiculous to assume, moreover, that the same Shakespeare texts will appeal to all pupils throughout England and Wales, or that the questions in the tests will draw out each pupil's best understanding and response. Particularly for this age group this is done most successfully through teacher assessment, rather than through timed tests which inevitably impose boring preparations on teacher and pupil. (It is, incidentally, deeply frustrating that, just when pupils have discovered the exciting modern film version of *Romeo and Juliet* starring Leonardo DiCaprio, the assessment authority is considering dropping this play from the Key Stage 3 list of set texts.)

Both in Britain and the United States successful teachers agree that active, investigative approaches must be central in the teaching of Shakespeare. Creative and imaginative writing, structured group work, classroom role-play, drama workshops and performance activities all aim to engage pupils fully in the plays. We want to recreate the exhilaration of the living theatre for our pupils. We do not want to repeat the boring exercises imposed on children in the classrooms of the 1930s. In addition, discursive writing assignments must not only promote close reading, but also encourage visualisation and criticism of productions in different historical and cultural contexts and in different media (e.g. live theatre, radio, film, CD-ROM). When tests lead to performance data which are used to judge a teacher's or a school's competence this kind of dynamic approach is in danger of being curtailed.

Fortunately, most English departments have not allowed the Shakespeare tests to dominate teaching. English teachers are struggling to keep Shakespeare active in the classroom. The pressure to improve scores in the Key Stage 3 tests does not help. At this stage of a child's development, teachers ought to be trusted to make their own judgements about pupils' understanding of, and response to, a Shakespeare text.

2. Grammar rules
In addition to the Shakespeare test, the Government has decreed that pupils' reading should be assessed through roughly 50 minutes' work on a couple of texts for Paper 1 (the remaining 40 minutes is a writing test). The main skill in

Paper 1 seems to be to 'support your ideas with words and phrases from the passage'. Aside from the danger of cultural bias (all texts being more familiar to some pupils rather than others), it is ludicrous to suppose that an accurate assessment of pupils' reading can be made from their performance in this simple test. Worse is yet to come, however, since the testing authority is proposing yet another change by insisting that knowledge of grammatical terminology be added to the items tested.

Teachers of English are completely committed to the teaching of grammar, but not to the kind of grammar that can be easily assessed in a short timed test. Studying language (including grammar) can be exciting and rewarding, but not when this is reduced to the naming of parts. The debate about the importance of knowledge about grammar is informed by prejudice and nostalgia for the kind of teaching which created so many semi-literate non-readers in the past. Educational research shows that the teaching of grammar in formal lessons does not necessarily improve the quality of writing or reading. Grammar is best taught in the context of the pupil's own writing and through an approach to texts which is exploratory rather than prescriptive.

The present tests already emphasise a particular way of reading texts which downplays pupils' personal responses and privileges analysis of character, plot and, especially, language. This is reflected in the fact that the word 'critical' does not appear in the National Curriculum for reading at Key Stages 3 and 4. An obsession with style rather than content (no doubt appropriate for government spin doctors) is an approach to reading that will not suit all readers. The proposed addition of grammatical terminology in the reading tests will exacerbate many pupils' sense of alienation from the reading process.

Never has there been a greater choice of high-quality literature for teenage readers; and never has there been such a concerted attempt by government agencies to narrow the definition of what it means to be a good reader. (It is ironic that this narrowness of vision on the part of one government department conflicts with the broader view promoted through the National Year of Reading by a different agency.) Tests necessarily dominate the curriculum, particularly when league tables determine the status of schools. Teachers know that it is simply not true that a movement up the league table necessarily reflects an improvement in pupils' reading abilities. Meanwhile the focus on testing discourages the development of ICT reading skills ....

Backs to the future

Tony Blair has gained much publicity from the Government's plans to link all schools through the Internet in a National Grid for Learning. It is disappointing, therefore, to see the Government firmly turning its back on the use of information and communication technology within the English curriculum by refusing to give teacher assessment its proper status. You cannot assess the ability to read CD-ROM information texts, or to read the Internet, through end-of-term tests. The more status these tests are given the less incentive English teachers will have to move reading into the next century.

This is a shame for we live in exciting times as far as reading goes. Douglas Adams recently launched his interactive video game, Starship Titanic, in which the players can hold conversations with the characters (typing in whatever text they want, to which the characters will reply); CD-ROMs and television programmes for children and teenagers experiment with increasingly complex and rapid combinations of visual and textual information; the world of work makes ever more demands on employees' ability to use information and communication technology. Yet none of this is supported by the National Curriculum for English (Reading) and its assessment arrangements which are backward-looking both in content and approach. We need a reading programme for the next century which values the complex reading skills involved in reading electronic media texts, not least because boys who are not interested in reading the literature of the past, or literature with an emotional landscape, may well choose to click off the reading menu being offered in the National Curriculum.

Can't read, won't read
Poor literacy in secondary schools is just as much about pupils who won't read as about pupils who can't read. Before the National Curriculum we understood this. Teachers used the term 'reluctant readers'. If progress is to be made in creating a more literate society we must start by valuing the texts that pupils enjoy, whether these be science fiction novels, football fanzines, role-play adventures, texts that represent the culture of the reader, whatever. This will not happen as long as teaching is dominated by a narrow, prescriptive choice of books, and the tests have the final say in defining pupils' achievements in reading.

And, finally, I have no doubt that parents and teachers would all agree that the money spent on these hugely expensive national tests would be put to better use providing more books for classroom and school library shelves.

Teaching disadvantaged readers
Paddy Lease

There are many reasons why adolescents may not have achieved literacy and unless teachers are aware of them, they cannot help. I cannot hope to mention them all and so will concentrate on those factors which I have most frequently encountered.

There may be fear, anxiety and expectation of failure. Some children have developed a fear of the written word and may even have severe anxiety attacks at the prospect of the dreaded reading lesson. 'Reading' for them has become a daunting experience, a torture rather than a pleasure. This is particularly so in group lessons and there is much to be gained by removing the child from the large group and making the reading period a comfortable, enjoyable one-to-one experience. If he or she is not singled out, and every class member has this special time, progress can be made. Obviously, the teacher cannot do this alone and I have had some success with training and using sympathetic sixth-formers as coaches, particularly when I could match the interests of coach and student. One tough, disaffected, rugby-mad young man began to read for pleasure through studying rugby books and newspaper articles with the captain of the First XV.

The teacher also has to be aware of the tensions of the group. Even in, or perhaps especially in, small special-needs groups of 10 to 14 pupils, there is tension, peer group pressure and fear of ridicule, but there is also an understanding that if one learns to read a little better one may be labelled an outsider by others in the group. There is also the constant fear of failing, of making a fool of oneself, yet again.

So, many disadvantaged youngsters decide that playing up, taking command of the situation or, at least, going along with the disrupters is the only way open to them. Motivating them so that they begin to get satisfaction from participation rather than disruption can open the door to much more. Even the most basic reward games can achieve this, as long as the teacher has established good basic control systems which enable interaction without chaos. Scrabble games with simple dictionaries and scores linked to chocolate rewards do wonders for arithmetic, as well as reading.

Sometimes there is such high expectation, even anticipation, of failure that all approaches are dismissed out of hand by the young person who says, 'You don't know. I know that I'm too stupid to learn. I can't do it. Many teachers before you have tried and failed'. This combination of defeatism, cynicism and false certainty can be difficult to overcome and may have to be dealt with before anything else can be achieved.

One quite successful approach to this kind of reading block is not to face it head on at all, not to hammer away at a youngster already hardened by experience so that he or she becomes ever more disenchanted and discouraged, more disinclined to learn and more bored with the whole process. It may be a cliché, but it is better to work on the child, not the problem. By giving the child attention and respect, by focusing on the child's hobbies, obsessions and enjoyments, the teacher can learn what is important to each individual and begin to provide material which the child finds relevant and interesting. Many a teacher scours public libraries for books on obscure topics, reads them to, and gradually with the student and then coaxes him or her into the library, helping that person to discover treasures he or she hadn't realised existed. One 14-year-old who had been labelled illiterate and who had been subjected to years of coaxing and special clinics began to read after he had addressed the group on his special interest – the breeding of tumbler pigeons – and had demonstrated the skills of his birds in the school playground. It took some time to find books on the subject and at first I simply read them to him, but as he corrected me, answered my amateurish questions and discussed points, his confidence grew and he gradually began to identify words and read for himself.

Often it is a matter of working from where the student is, be it *Star Trek*, guns, motor mechanics or tumbler pigeons, and not from where you wish he was or where you want to be. In *My Family and other Animals* Gerald Durrell says of one teacher: 'At once my enthusiastic but haphazard interest in nature became focused for I found that by writing things down I could learn and remember much more. The only mornings that I was ever on time for my lessons were those which were given up to natural history'.

I am reminded of the saying that you have to get on the bus at your own bus stop, not at the bus stop you wish that you were standing at.

Another problem is apathy. There has always been apathy towards learning, but in the present age it is by no means fashionable to list reading as a past-time. It is not always seen as necessary, let alone admirable. Once pupils have mastered the ability to recognise words and sentences they may decide they want nothing more from reading. Many young people hardly read at all, except for the occasional fan magazine, and dislike those 'boring' lessons where they are forced to do so. When they want information they turn to computers, television and videos. Many teachers 'trot out' *Kes* or *Lord of the Flies* or sit their classes in front of the television, lesson after lesson, and are surprised by their pupils' lack of enthusiasm. What the teacher needs to do is demonstrate how relevant the written word is to the interests and needs of young people. They may be convinced that books are for cissies or old fogeys: well, introduce the scramble biker to biking books; maintenance manuals and accounts of thrills and spills; or show the computer games buff how to access the information banks on the Internet.

Sometimes the problem stems from the fact that there is little or no encouragement in the home. Many young people belong to families where there are no books and no tradition of, or respect for reading. They may not be given time or opportunity for reading; there may be no quiet place set aside – no encouragement. Other activities are always deemed to be more important. There may even be active discouragement. Books may be returned unopened or damaged. A child may report that a book has been destroyed or thrown in a bin and, on one occasion, I was informed that Dad and the dog had been playing with a book and the dog had eaten it.

It is possible to develop a higher level of literacy in children by providing (a) libraries and study areas where books can be read and homework completed and (b) tutors and sympathetic adults who can encourage, answer questions and build confidence. Many schools do this. However, support has to continue when these students reach the higher levels of education. For me, this meant the provision of suggested reading lists and stimulating books, debates and discussion groups, liberal and cultural study courses, and a varied programme of theatre, cinema, museum visits, lectures and poetry sessions.

A word of warning is needed, however. The film *Educating Rita* showed only too clearly what can happen when a family feels threatened by the developing literacy of one of its members. Labouring to make a young person literate without a basic understanding (a) of the whole situation (b) of the strengths and weaknesses of the student and (c) of the possible consequences of one's actions can cause more serious problems than the ones that the teacher is attempting to solve. One sixth-former became increasingly alienated from her family as a result of her new-found interests to such an extent that she had to leave home and live in a bedsitter found for her by the school. Since then, she has had to deal with feelings of isolation and insecurity which were, at least in part, the result of being uprooted from one environment and not successfully transplanting into another.

In most cases a student's illiteracy or semi-literacy can be traced to a lack of stimulation. In the early stages, a child who is reluctant to read will be stimulated by being read to, by being bombarded with interesting or exciting material until he or she comes to expect and depend upon a regular intake of words. Storytelling, as most parents know only too well, not only keeps children quiet and tranquillises them for bedtime, but also stimulates their imaginations, increases their vocabularies, broadens their horizons and encourages them to satisfy their growing appetites by finding and reading books for themselves. A young friend of mine who was introduced to storytelling tapes before he was three years old was creeping out of bed at 6 a.m. to switch the tapes on for himself by the time he was four, was demanding and collecting first the tapes and then the books by the time he was five, and then reading the books for himself when tapes were not available. Aged 12, he has just won a year-group competition for The Most Imaginative Story, telling us all 'I was just carried away on my enthusiasm'.

So, as usual, it all depends on the teacher. The most successful teacher will appreciate the value of literacy; will love the written and spoken word and be capable of infecting his or her charges with that enthusiasm; will take time to understand the needs and circumstances of students; will be adaptable and persistent, providing appropriate, relevant and interesting material, and will stimulate, encourage and guide them and ultimately launch them into the world of words.

Reading at ages 14 to 16

Anne Barnes

Literacy is the buzz word for the late-1990s. Everybody approves of it but what exactly is it? Many teachers, engaged daily in the business of exploring with their pupils the ideas which are presented in different sorts of texts, are bemused by the sudden advent of literacy as a subject in itself. They know that teachers of all subjects and at all stages, are involved in the pursuit of literacy whether they are greeting 5-year-olds in the reception class or preparing students for GCSE. It is not something which can be simply slotted into a daily hour routine or promoted by slimming down other parts of the curriculum in order to find more time for spelling and grammar exercises. Literacy, of course, is like riding a bicycle – it is an expression of confidence. You start off wobbling along with someone running behind to help you keep your balance, then suddenly you take off on your own. Both the early skill of recognising words on the page and the later, more sophisticated skill of deconstructing a complex literary text, depend on the confidence which is built up by what has already been achieved, what satisfaction that achievement has brought and the way it relates to individual experience. During the teenage years, as this bicycle gets bigger, the confidence sometimes wobbles again and reading skills get stuck, particularly in the Key Stage 4 years leading to GCSE.

At this stage the English teacher tries to sustain confidence and interest by using two balancing strategies. First, it is necessary to provide the opportunity for detailed study and analysis of a particular text. It must be interesting to a person going through the stages of adolescence, but more importantly, must provide enough ideas, interesting use of language, narrative or dramatic techniques or other particular features to be really worth studying. It might be *Macbeth* or it might be *A View from the Bridge*. It could be *Silas Marner* or *Roll of Thunder, Hear My Cry*. It does not have to be an accepted part of what is vaguely called the English Literary Heritage, nor does it have to be in timeless prose (or poetry). It simply has to be accessible to students who want to stretch out to read something they might not have come across otherwise and to practise their critical skills through close study. Confidence comes from the detail of the study and the need to know a text so well that it becomes a benchmark, or perhaps a symbol of initiation into a new way of looking.

The second thing the English teacher aims to do is to help the student to extend the range of reading from which they derive pleasure and interest. For many students this is a sort of treasure trail by which they are led on from one book to another. Each successful 'read' will contain hints as to where to look next; so the teacher's job is to help to pick these hints up and, through their own wide reading, suggest where they might lead. For other students it is more complicated, perhaps because they have enjoyed one book so much that they keep looking for another exactly similar and so are always disappointed. In that case the trail goes cold and the teacher must step in. Perhaps in the classroom it is more a question of a triangle than a trail. At one point of this triangle is the student's stage of maturity, interest and ability; at another is the book they have just been enjoying, and at the third corner is the teacher's idea of the sort of book these two earlier angles combine to suggest. In a successful triangle the three points have a clear relation to each other, although sometimes there is an unexpected straggliness with broken lines connecting the points.

Life between the ages of 14 and 16 can be very confusing and, since everyone around seems to be relentlessly pushing one on towards adult behaviour, it is sometimes a help to be able to collapse in private into childhood reading. It is not unknown in the classroom for a girl who appears to be writing an essay on fate in *Tess of the D'Urbevilles* to be actually reading Enid Blyton's *First Term at Mallory Towers* under the desk. Nor is it particularly surprising if a boy who has just spent an evening defining the nature of the comedy in *Much Ado About Nothing*, chooses Richmal Crompton or Roald Dahl for a bit of quick bedtime reading. Nevertheless, this kind of regression does rather panic teachers, particularly in the present climate when linear progression from one stage to another is all the rage and development is being caged into levels and grades by examination mark schemes and curriculum statements. What should teachers do? Should they, in the GCSE years, simply ignore the childish reading baggage which their students bring with them and the popular Jackie Collins-style fiction which they find in their parents' airport baggage. Or should they attempt to harness the pleasures and skills developed through these fairly mindless texts in order to enrich the reaching forward into a varied and more rewarding literary diet? This can only be answered on an individual basis and often has to be thought out with each student in turn. It is particularly important at the GCSE stage because this should be the moment, between the current constraints imposed by Key Stage 3 assessment and the focused rigour of A Level, when stretching out, extending the range and discovering personal tastes should be possible.

In the past it was possible. Enlightened GCSE dual-certification syllabuses (for English and English Literature) between 1987 and 1993 required students to produce a folder of work which contained writing about different aspects of poetry, prose and drama texts, and an extended essay on their own individual reading. They were required to make comparisons between texts, to write both creatively and critically and – for the higher grades – to show some knowledge about language. No set texts were specified so teachers and students together could select pieces written about whatever texts had been studied during the two-year course. The folders were marked first by the teacher responsible for each student, then by the group of teachers in that school department together, and then by external moderators. During the few years while this system was in operation a remarkable expertise in assessment developed among English teachers which contributed to their professional development as a whole and influenced the way they organised their teaching at every age level.

Just as the work done for GCSE was showing a significant rise in standards across all levels of ability and every type of school, these enabling coursework syllabuses were snatched away and replaced by others, in which a large proportion of the assessment was done through externally marked examination papers and only a small amount allowed for coursework. Now, five years later, we are embarking on yet another set of syllabuses, where the proportion of coursework remains the same but the requirements for the examinations have been made much more specific. Although the range of reading which is required – both for English and English Literature – appears to have been extended, it has actually narrowed down the possibilities for many schools. Students now have to show evidence of having read both twentieth-century and pre-twentieth-century prose, poetry and drama and to have studied the media in some form. Different examination boards have arranged this differently but on the whole these various types of reading are tested through the exam papers. Work on Shakespeare is examined though coursework in all the boards' syllabuses, as is wider reading and also (for most boards) study of the media. The other areas both in English and English Literature are assessed by random examination questions.

The only way these requirements could be made manageable was for the examination boards to provide anthologies for candidates to study which would enable them to cover all the areas required and on which examination questions could be set. Although this may be convenient and perhaps the only solution to this problem, it is also absurd. Do we really want these slim anthologies to decide which poems will be studied by all the nation's 16-year-olds, instead of giving the teachers scope to search out the poems which will have most impact in their own particular classrooms? Wordsworth's 'Daffodils' is all very well in itself, but the thought of it becoming a sort of national chant is a dispiriting one.

Another consequence of the present tightly constructed GCSE syllabuses is that teachers feel the pressure of time acutely and are tempted to fall back on short stories – particularly to fulfil the pre-twentieth-century prose category – or to look around for abridged versions which their students can take in quickly. In the past, the GCSE years often provided pupils – particularly those who were only partly hooked on reading fiction – with their first chance to read a long novel together and to see how the many parts of a complex narrative fitted together to make a whole. Although the opportunity to study a long novel is still there in theory, it is becoming increasingly rare in practice.

It is sad to see how the original vision of a national curriculum has been corroded and overtaken by the panic about assessment. Now, in Key Stages 1 and 2, we have a National Literacy Strategy, which puts the emphasis on a narrower range of experiences and skills and is elbowing the National Curriculum into the background. At the same time, the Teacher Training Agency has prescribed what student teachers should be taught – thereby indirectly setting up another alternative curriculum. In Key Stage 3, the externally marked examination paper which tests the pupil's knowledge of a prescribed Shakespeare play, has already distorted the curriculum in a way undreamt of by the original committee which sat down to devise a flexible and rigorous curriculum. The reading and writing tests, which are being piloted this year, look set to further intimidate teachers into drilling their pupils to jump through uncontextualised grammatical hoops.

It might be thought that having made it to the end of the Key Stage 3 assault course, students need space to explore, to find out about their own tastes in reading and their own ways of relating to that reading. But having emerged from Key Stage 3 they enter a course dominated by a slightly different but no less inhibiting assessment system. The cramping effect of the present structure on the reading which is done in the secondary school has not yet had time to fully show up during A Level, but soon it will become clear that today's students are not so well equipped to start their A Level courses now as were those students who were brought up through the opportunities and disciplines of the old coursework syllabuses.

The change in general attitude towards English teaching has been quite dramatic over the last 10 years and sometimes the new ways are beguiling. We all want higher standards of literacy. We may welcome a National Literacy Strategy at primary and secondary level if it provides a framework which can be studied and then adapted to individual situations, becoming a reference point but never a strait-jacket. However, teachers know that whatever detailed work goes into constructing a scheme of work, it can only ever be a small part of the story. We may need schemes, strategies and businesslike plans of skills to give us a sense of direction, but we do not need irrelevantly precise assessment grids to make sure we all end up in the same place. Students, above all, need space to develop the confidence to move from one stage to another, to form their own opinions about what is true and valuable against what is shoddy and shallow in texts of all sorts. Perhaps the National Year of Reading can help to provide that space – and that confidence.

Sixth-form studies
Jane Ogborn

Superficially, A Level – or at least A Level English Literature – doesn't look very different today from the way it looked 30 years ago; much the same number and kinds of set books, chosen for the students by the teacher, and written about almost entirely in timed examinations. The set books texts are still drawn mainly from the great names of English literature, women writers are in the minority and writing by authors from cultures other than white British, or texts written during the past 10 years, are so few and far between they are almost invisible. But during the past 20 years there have been changes in choices for students, in expectations of them and in the assessment of their work. The two former are great improvements and have significant implications for developing students' reading, in the widest sense; the last could have been, if the politicians hadn't thought they knew best.

Students in 1998, choosing to continue with English after GCSE, now have several options besides English Literature. Oral and written communication skills will be essential elements in any GNVQ course, and at AS and A Level, they can choose from Literature, Language, or a syllabus offering a combination of the two, all possibly through modular courses. They might also opt for A Level Communications, Media Studies, Drama or Theatre Studies. At AS and A Level expectations of post-16 students and their reading are rightly high. The subject 'cores' developed by the Qualifications and Curriculum Authority (QCA) specify what syllabuses must cover, in terms of knowledge and skills as well as lists of texts. These make it clear that Literature and Language courses are intended to induct students into the disciplines of the study of these subjects: not just knowing the content of a handful of books, but also understanding and applying relevant concepts and analytical approaches. So in Literature they are expected to read demanding prose, poetry and drama texts, written before and after the arbitrarily chosen date of 1900, to understand about the contexts in which these texts were produced and know something of the literary traditions which influenced their authors. In Language they are expected to be able to analyse and evaluate how language works in a wide variety of spoken and written texts. They are expected to recognise that texts are consciously constructed and be able to comment in an informed way about the choices which writers make in doing this. Students today are expected to have views of their own, be able to make judgements about what they read, and have a developed sense of themselves as readers.

The most significant developments in A Level Literature examinations began in the late 1970s with the creation of the popular and innovative AEB 660 syllabus. This allowed schools or colleges to choose for themselves some of the texts studied, suiting them to the interests of particular student groups. It encouraged students' independent reading by requiring a 2,000 to 3,000-word essay on two or three texts, preferably of a student's own choice. The students' folders of writing about their reading beyond the texts set for the final examinations were assessed by their teachers and contributed a third of the marks to their final result. The extended essay quickly became recognised as a major element in a young person's development as a reader and writer. Students of all abilities gained confidence from completing this substantial piece of independent work. More importantly, they were encouraged to explore beyond their set texts to find new kinds of reading for themselves. The result was an increase of interest in literatures alongside, and other than, the English literary heritage – black American and British writing, post-colonial literatures, writing by women and contemporary writing of all kinds – on which students could exercise their own developing critical skills without relying on a body of received critical opinion. The early 1980s also saw the development of A Level English Language examinations, either independent from or in conjunction with Literature. As part of focusing students' attention on how language works, these courses extended students' reading to a much wider range of kinds of text, including literature as one variety of language alongside journalism, travel writing, information, polemic and so on. Just as the extended essay on literature fostered students' reading and their critical skills, practical investigations and personal research into language helped students to develop their analytical abilities. In both cases, the fact that this work involved an element of choice, was produced for a folder of coursework and not in an examination, and carried an appropriate proportion of the total marks, were all essential differences from previous – or indeed, current – syllabuses.

The other really significant change that has taken place since these syllabuses were created is in many teachers' approaches to A Level work. The new syllabuses developed partly as a result of teachers' increasing interest in, and knowledge of, critical theory and linguistics. For literature, probably the most significant lessons have been learned from an eclectic mix of post-structuralism and reader response theory – increasing awareness of how texts work, combined with the understanding that none of us reads the same text as anyone else, for reasons of our background, education, gender, race, age, nationality and so on. Consequently, there can be no single correct interpretation of any text, which the teacher teaches and the student learns. Some people deride the results of this understanding as 'personal response', mistakenly assuming that it means that in discussions of texts 'anything goes' and that half-baked ideas which are not based on careful reading are accepted as just as valid as one that has been thoroughly thought out. But isn't a personal response exactly what any mature reader – certainly any critic – voices when they talk or write about a text? Today, good A Level teaching is as much about helping students to learn how to read – what questions to ask, which ideas to follow up, what comparisons to draw with other texts that have been read – and develop well informed responses to their reading, as it is about transmitting information about books.

So, if all these changes have been going on at A Level, what's the problem? Simply this. In 1991, the then Prime Minister, John Major, decided, without looking at any of the evidence to the contrary, that there was far too much assessment of coursework going on, and that it should be stopped. It is ironic that at much the same time the members of the Department of English in the University of Cambridge were deciding that they would make coursework a compulsory element in their assessment at degree level, because of the value which they could see it had for encouraging students' reading. The GCSE syllabuses, which had only been examined since 1989, have been rewritten twice since then – once in 1992 to restrict the amount of written coursework and make final examinations compulsory, and again in 1995, following the revision of the National Curriculum. A Level syllabuses were also rewritten in 1994, to bring them in line with the reductions in coursework at GCSE. More changes to A Level syllabuses, which will entirely alter the relationship between AS and A Levels, but will retain the same proportions of coursework and examinations, are currently on hold, waiting for government decisions about the shape of education and qualifications post 16. Each rewriting has moved both GCSE and A Level further away from frameworks which encouraged wide and independent reading, and limited the possibilities for teachers to tailor reading to individual students, open up new areas of interest and pleasure for them and allow them a freer hand in the choice of some texts for study. At the same time, QCA and the subject 'cores' make the syllabuses more explicit about the types of texts to be read and the ways in which those texts should be approached.

This is not a criticism of the A Level subject cores as descriptions of what Literature and Language study ought to look like post 16. But if A Level students are to analyse and evaluate texts, and show understanding of the contexts in which they were written and of the literary traditions to which they belong, they need a broad experience of reading all kinds of different sorts of text. They also need to have begun to find their feet as readers who are developing their own tastes. The National Curriculum Orders for English which prescribe what children should be taught between the ages of 5 and 16, and the GCSE and A Level syllabuses which lay down how their knowledge and understanding is to be assessed, map out the reading landscape over which post-16 English studies should be able to range with confidence. They see the child as making a fairly unproblematic journey from acquiring the basic skills of reading from 5 to 7, then exercising them on an increasing variety of texts between 7 and 14, and finally arriving at full maturity as an independent and confident reader at 16 and beyond. Unfortunately, just as studying a map never entirely prepares you for the realities of the journey, most students' reading experiences are inevitably going to be a limited version of this ideal programme. The current GCSE English syllabuses insist that every aspect of the range of reading specified in the National Curriculum must be seen to be assessed: Shakespeare, literature written before 1900 by well-known English writers, literature written after 1900, non-literary materials, media texts, and texts from other cultures. No one would argue against introducing children to all these kinds of texts, but it is resulting in an unbalanced diet of reading for GCSE English – please note, English not Literature – where literary texts threaten to monopolise attention and teaching time at the expense of non-fiction and non-literary texts, information of all kinds, journalism, debate, polemic, a range of media texts, and so on. These are the texts that students wishing to study English Language at A Level – or, even more importantly, those who will be adults in the twenty-first century – need to be able to read critically and confidently, but in GCSE English they are largely relegated to the source materials for end-of-course exam questions. What is even worse, with so much literary reading demanded by the syllabuses, there is the risk of tokenism setting in. Granted this is a worst-case scenario, but it would be perfectly possible for a student to arrive on an A Level course having read only a Shakespeare play, a couple of short stories, and a handful of poems during their GCSE course. If they have been entered for GCSE Literature as well, as many still are, there will be some continuity in the sorts of texts read, and the kinds of work they are expected to do with them, including learning about historical, social and cultural contexts of texts, but if they want to study A Level Language, they will not have had the same amount of experience of other equally important kinds of reading.

All this is not a criticism of the range of reading specified in the National Curriculum. But it is a criticism of recent political decisions about assessment and the effect that has on teaching and learning, and on reading. A Level teachers have probably always thought that students didn't read enough, and they put considerable effort and imagination into encouraging them to read more. What we need at GCSE and post 16 are assessment systems which make more space for individual choice, and encourage students to apply what they are learning about language and about texts to books which speak to them – culturally and personally. In his review of post-16 provision, Sir Ron Dearing emphasised the need for all courses to give students opportunities to develop the key skills of communication, application of number and Information Technology, independent learning, working with others and problem solving. Apart from application of number, all these are directly relevant to English studies, but the new syllabuses make it much harder for teachers to go on encouraging the kinds of extended independent research and project work previously developed through extended essays on literary texts or investigative work on language. When an assessment system permits, it is perfectly possible, and indeed highly desirable, to combine in a Literature course the detailed study of canonical texts with the freedom to choose other areas of reading on which students can exercise their skills of analysis and comparison. Through this kind of work, and through any work on language which integrates reading and writing about that reading, students learn to select, discriminate, and sustain their reading over time and across a body of material in ways which the concentrated study of single texts, or comparing pieces of text under exam conditions, cannot do. But the time it takes, and the value it has for the student, have to be adequately reflected in the weight it has within the whole assessment system.

The best thing we can ask for for future students of language and literature are GCSE English courses which genuinely encourage and reward reading of all sorts of texts, with Literature offered to the maximum number of candidates as a complementary subject for study. Post 16, we should be aiming for all students to graduate from A Level or other courses, not just having read things other people have chosen for them, but also as real readers of the texts they will continue to choose for themselves.

Reading and the university
Judy Simons

What has he to do with books?' enquires Jane Austen's Emma of Harriet Smith, attempting to discredit Robert Martin's suitability as a husband.[1] Her question is an important one. Its multiple ironies work against Emma, the grand inquisitor, in her assumptions of intellectual superiority, whilst at the same time proving her point. For Mr Martin's eclectic reading habits (which include the Agricultural Reports *and The Vicar of Wakefield*) reveal him as a man of good sense who reads both for information and for self-improvement. Astonishingly to Emma, if not to the practised Austen reader, Mr Martin also writes 'a very good letter'. His proposal of marriage is not merely grammatically accurate but so lucid, articulate and sensitively phrased that Emma has difficulty in believing that a young farmer, lacking the benefits of a classical education, could possibly have written it unaided.

The relationship between the experience of reading and what is now fashionably referred to in education-speak as 'transferable skills', that is, its spin-off in understanding, communicative abilities and independent thinking, comes as no surprise to those of us who teach in modern universities. A recent survey of university English conducted by the Council for College and University English (CCUE) across the spread of UK Higher Education institutions, shows academics as virtually unanimous – a remarkable state of affairs in itself – in identifying the benefits of a literary education.[2] Indeed, the diversity of the HE syllabus masks significant agreement on the definition of the core skills expected of English undergraduates. Whether they are reading *Beowulf* or Barthes, Matthew Lewis or C. S. Lewis, students are expected to emerge with an understanding of discrete subject methodologies and a solid grounding in the historical, intellectual and cultural contexts of literature. Professors of English stand united in their conviction that the experience of reading in a professional, scholarly environment should equip graduates with high-level analytic skills, the capacity for critical reasoning, self-reflection and conceptual grasp, together with the ability to learn autonomously and to exercise flexibility of mind. However resistible we might find it, the new terminology which guides us towards thinking of literature in terms of the skills it transmits does indeed focus the mind on why we teach what we teach, and just what it is that students learn.

For, ever more frequently we are asked to justify the teaching of reading in a technologically oriented world. And the notion of what constitutes literary 'value' has shifted radically from the Leavisite understanding of that term in order to adapt to a new academic culture that prioritises employability over moral improvement. An enlightening footnote to the debate is that, when asked to rank its relative merit, 79 per cent of academics surveyed felt that the ability to engage in discussion of ethical values still remains an essential or desirable outcome of studying English; only 4 per cent suggested that it was of no relevance whatsoever. The Blairite agenda clearly has a long way to go before it penetrates British university thinking about the purposes of a degree in the Humanities.

Yet it remains vital that we continue to remind ourselves and our students that the 'value' of literature extends way beyond mere functionalism to release an awareness of the expressive resources of language and the intellectual flexibility which is its natural accompaniment. This is the true purpose of the curriculum; what drives its design and determines the choices our students confront. But how is that purpose fulfilled by the textual content? If it is indeed the case that whether we teach Romantic poetry or Afro-American writing we are pursuing the same end product, does it, in fact, matter what goes into the syllabus? While academics might concur as to what we are about, the precise design of the curriculum is probably what inspires the most heated academic debate among proponents of radically different pedagogic and critical positions: Samuel Richardson or Dorothy Richardson; E. M. or Margaret Forster? Does the jostling for priority amongst the reading lists mean that George Eliot and T. S. are inevitably in competition? In the modular frameworks, which now determine course structures for 90 per cent of English degrees, is there opportunity for undergraduates to read as widely as they or their tutors might like? Alternatively (and some might find this the more burning issue), is there still space for tutors to direct students to what they think is good for them? Are, in fact, the two incompatible?

In Anthony Powell's epic work *A Dance to the Music of Time*, that exemplar of twentieth-century Philistinism, Widmerpool, points out the dangers of reading modern literature. 'It doesn't do to read too much ... You get to look at life with a false perspective. By all means have some familiarity with the standard authors. I should never raise any objection to that. But it is no good clogging your mind with a lot of trash from modern novels'.[3]

Five years ago, *The Times Higher Education Supplement* greeted with relish the news that Shakespeare was no longer compulsory reading for English undergraduates. At about the same time, the 'Angela Carter syndrome' gained notoriety, as the British Academy reported that it received more applications to fund English doctoral research on Carter than on the literature of the entire sixteenth, seventeenth and eighteenth centuries put together. Both statements were received as irrefutable evidence of a decline in standards; that a degree in English was rapidly losing both its intellectual rigour and its street cred. And this is in spite of the widely held view that Angela Carter is one of the most textually sophisticated and critically elusive of contemporary authors, her work never less than intellectually demanding in its modernity; a contradiction in terms according to Widmerpool.

Widmerpool might deplore what the 1990s university has to offer, but dons themselves celebrate their eclectic stance. Most English degrees, committed to the principle of diversity, now offer an impressive range of core and option structures. And among the options, women's writing of all periods has become the most popular choice, just beating Shakespeare into second place. Contemporary writing and American literature follow closely at their heels. We need to be careful in evaluating the significance of such statistics. The figures should not in themselves be taken to indicate that there is a progressive 'dumbing down' of English degrees. Whilst Shakespeare might appear to be the second favourite from students' option choices, with 44 mentions in the popularity stakes, this must be placed in context. Shakespeare is only optional in 44 institutions; the others make the study of Shakespeare compulsory. Women's writing, on the other hand, is mandatory in only two institutions. So the fact that it receives 49 votes in the CCUE count of the top 10 most popular modules is less remarkable than might be supposed, especially given that the majority of undergraduates enrolled on English degree programmes are themselves women, seeking their own critical location in the literary canon.

Certainly the 1998 CCUE survey produces some surprises about the modern study of university English. Not the least of these is the apparent erosion of the old binary divide between the traditional universities and the ex-public-sector-funded institutions (now euphemistically re-named as 'new' universities) in terms of their underlying course philosophy. Resources are of course another matter: the sacred Oxbridge individual tutorial is a privilege denied those students who attend 'workshops' of 30 or more in the poverty-stricken ex-polytechnics. Yet there is no apparent immediate correlation between the type of university and the nature of the undergraduate English syllabus. Renaissance poetry, Victorian fiction, and Modernist literature remain the staple diet of students' official reading. Spenser, the Brontës and Joyce seem perfectly comfortable working in harmony with the post-colonial writing, Irish literature and early American literature, which are all rising stars in today's curriculum. That very juxtaposition creates intellectual challenges. For while the familiar names and titles are still prominent, they don't necessarily appear in the same packages as 20 or 30 years ago.

This is not merely a question of gaudy wrapping paper. Most courses now operate on a 'core' and options model, and it is the textual shopping trolley filled with dazzling option choices which reveals most strikingly how cutting-edge research invigorates teaching. It is not that the canonical works of English literature are out of favour, but rather that they appear in an imaginative reconfiguration of fresh and mutually illuminating contexts. A module on detective fiction might feature Edgar Allen Poe, Dorothy L. Sayers and Raymond Chandler, as well as *Bleak House* and *The Moonstone*. 'Literature and Christianity' permits *The Pilgrim's Progress* to rub shoulders with *The Scarlet Letter* and with Golding's *The Spire*. Similarly eighteenth-century fiction, which rarely appears in its once familiar 'Rise of the Novel' clothing, will surface in a series of guises: *Northanger Abbey* and *The Mysteries of Udolpho* in a course on 'Literature of Terror'; *Robinson Crusoe* and *Humphry Clinker* in 'Narratives of Travel'. It is when these standard works are read alongside their non-canonical counterparts, such as *Silence of the Lambs*, or *Oroonoko*, *The Voyage of the Beagle* and Jamaica Kincaid, that the conjunction creates a dialogue that actively interrogates the interface between the popular and the classical, the literary and the non-literary. Lycra has infiltrated the historical corset of university English teaching. Generic and theoretical perspectives have breathed fresh air and new life into the periodicity in which course design was once enshrined.

As a result our students are no longer passive receptors of the great works, Widmerpool's 'standard authors', but creative participants in the act of reading, using literature to test concepts of canonicity, the history of criticism, the meaning of genre, and the parameters of the subject. Whatever their working conditions or the nature of their student cohort, the vast majority of academics defend to the hilt the diversity of our current university provision. It is this which facilitates the freedom to develop new materials, inspires the willingness to propose new challenges and release new energies within the subject, factors which are essential to the dynamism and health of the discipline and the consequent attainment of graduate skills.

As the data gathered from the CCUE survey demonstrates, and not incompatible with the principle of diversity, there is also a strong but previously unrecognised convergence from institution to institution and course to course in what is offered. There is no area of writing in English and Old English which does not have a strong representation across the provision as a whole, and although it is relatively rare to find a 'new' university offering mediaeval literature, it is by no means unknown. In fact the typical foundation year for first-year students in the 'new', traditional and university college sectors shares much common ground. Eighty-seven per cent of university English courses insist on practical criticism and 79 percent on literary theory, as a basis from which to proceed. Critical practice and its theoretical frameworks – interestingly in that priority order – are now perceived as the bedrock of an advanced education in English, where the ability to read closely is developed through an understanding of the conceptual models which shape that exercise. We aim to produce self-aware readers, whose textual engagement is compounded by an enquiry into its historical, linguistic, philosophical and political determinants. Effectively then, wherever they are educated, students are required to question and debate their own assumptions about the reading process, a process which is strengthened by the seminar experience, which has now taken over from the lecture as the central method of course delivery.

The convergence of opinion about the curriculum should not be confused with blandness of intent. There is a widely-shared concern that the range of literature taught should not shrink to a handful of periods or genres. Overwhelmingly university teachers of English in the UK are opposed to the introduction of a national curriculum, of any external body determining what should be taught on a university syllabus. This is not merely a self-defensive stance from which academics jealously guard their entrenched position. Rather the overall pattern of curriculum provision displays a degree of coherence which grows from shared practice and a set of common assumptions which permit innovation, development and challenge. When asked directly, only five respondents thought that the diversity of provision definitely represented 'a worrying indication of unstable standards and a fragmenting discipline'. [4]

For what is taught and what is learned through reading English at university are not necessarily identical. While university teachers insist on autonomy and academic freedom, they are also fighting for the fact that an English degree programme cannot be reduced to a series of set books. There is a remarkable dissonance between the terminology dons employ in describing their programmes for official inspection to quality assessors from the Funding Council or the Quality Agency, and the language they use in discussing their courses with their peers. Responses to the CCUE survey were refreshing in their frankness. In answer to the question, 'Do you think that there should be a common core to the HE English curriculum?' several remarked that we already had one. Only one respondent was in favour of a set curriculum, and then 'only if I can set it!'

Rather the literary syllabus is a stimulus, which enables students to explore further, to inculcate a sense of enquiry and imaginative excitement that is uncontainable in any official description of a course module. Academics in the modern university are continually being urged by external scrutineers or by their own 'curriculum development centres' to provide descriptors of course units in the educational jargon of today: with aims, objectives, exemplary content and a guarantee of learning outcomes. These 'learning outcomes' are in their turn subjected to scrutiny, evaluated against a further set of 'performance indicators', so that litigious students can turn round and justifiably blame their professors for having failed to provide them with the upper second which the course descriptors virtually guaranteed. Widmerpool would undoubtedly approve.

But what does a degree in English mean? It is undoubtedly the case that English remains one of the most popular of university subjects. Over 30,000 students are currently studying English in universities, either for a single Honours degree or as part of a joint or combined Honours route. This represents about 5 per cent of the total undergraduate enrolment in all subjects in all institutions. Indeed, English is the third most popular subject in British Higher Education. Only Computer Science and Business Management attract more students.[5]

Clearly this indicates that there is something anomalous in a system where current government directives emphasise the need for the vocational and professional orientation of university courses and fund them accordingly. Ask students why they choose English and very few will answer in terms of a specific career objective. Rather students do English for the same reason they have always done it – the sheer enjoyment of reading.

There is still a danger that the inexorable march of the new late-twentieth century, encouraged by the Blairite agenda, will reduce 'Literature', its consumption and production, to a petrified fossil. The 'standard authors' in Widmerpool's phrase, are fixed inexorably, immovable, identified by a consensus of what constitutes a cultural inheritance. As the hero of Powell's novel and himself the author of a modern novel, itself a 'classic' of modern fiction (which, incidentally, hardly any young person in the 1990s has read), Nicholas Jenkins stands as a dynamic counterpoint to Widmerpool's egregious crassness. Jenkins thus becomes an embodiment of the artist's role as a recorder, observer and illuminator of contemporary mores, and his view of the march of the twentieth century towards intellectual determinism is truly prophetic.

The tension between these standpoints is one that today's universities confront. Yet that sense of intellectual excitement which students bring to academic reading is a huge advantage for us as university teachers. While some die-hard university dons continue to see a core of literature itself as a defensible aim of a traditional English degree, the vast majority prefer to use that primary enjoyment of the text as a means to an end. The design of the syllabus is then a crucial means of harnessing the pleasure of reading to productive purpose, even though most academics are characteristically reluctant to admit to engaging in any activity that suggests complicity with rather than healthy dissent from government agendas. Yet when pushed, 60.5 per cent of respondents in the CCUE survey were willing to countenance a description of the subject as at least in part concerned with the transmission of 'skills'. All were emphatic that these skills were embedded within the English curriculum itself. They were also keen to stress that turning out well-qualified and highly skilled graduates who are employable is not the same thing as bowing to what many in the profession perceive as external pressure to conflate 'education' and 'training'. Academics are genuinely anxious that the subject should not be reduced to narrow or vocationally-oriented perspectives which could stifle the imagination, creativity, originality and empathy which are seen as essential outcomes of current curricular models. Literature is not a dead or useless subject out of touch with the modern environment. Nor is the study of contemporary literature a sign that we ignore the values of the past and its sophisticated lessons. Despite Widmerpool's nervousness about 'modern novels', the concept of a dynamic and up-to-date literary curriculum, which is responsive to students' needs, is intimately linked with the mature, independent graduates who are its products.

Throughout *Emma*, as indeed in much of her work, Jane Austen alerts us to the centrality of reading in the creation of a whole person, the dangers of intellectual pretentiousness, and the cultural capital invested in evaluating reading practices. We must not assume that one form of reading, the classical inheritance of high art, is necessarily superior to another. The popular novel, as the caustic narrator of *Northanger Abbey* is quick to remind us, displays 'the greatest powers of the mind ... the most thorough knowledge of human nature ... [and] the liveliest effusions of wit and humour ... conveyed to the world in the best chosen language',[6] despite its being the butt of reviewers' scorn, and the Agricultural Reports are absolutely the right reading matter for a young gentleman farmer. Austen's *Emma*, nonetheless, also recognises a further significant dimension of the function of reading, implicit in her interrogation: that a developed culture establishes sophisticated hierarchies of reading together with a series of complex value judgements about capability – whether for marriage or for working in the Civil Service – which accompany them. We should not fall into the trap of accepting preconceived judgements about textual subject or literary period without understanding the theoretical debates which frame and problematise university reading practices. It is these debates which engender the intellectual liveliness which characterises our graduates. At the same time it is not coincidental that graduates who have read widely emerge with an impressive and dextrous collection of high-level skills which equip them to enter a wide variety of professions.

Perhaps we just ought to tell them so more clearly.

Notes

1   Jane Austen, 1815, *Emma*, chap. 4
2   Rick Rylance, Judy Simons and Vincent Gillespie, *The English Curriculum: Diversity and Standards*, Council for College and University English (Bristol: University of the West of England, 1998)
3   Anthony Powell (1951), *A Dance to the Music of Time:* vol. 1, *A Question of Upbringing*, p. 134 (London: Mandarin, 1997)
4   Rylance et al., ibid., p. 6
5   Statistics given are taken from the most recently published HESA data (1996) and the UCAS Annual Report (1995)
6   Jane Austen, 1818, *Northanger Abbey*, chap. 5

Notes on contributors

ANNE BARNES taught English at Holland Park Comprehensive School in West London for many years. She has taken part in research projects concerned with assessment and is a Principal Examiner for NEAB GCSE English. Since 1991, she has been the General Secretary of the National Association for the Teaching of English.

SVEN BIRKERTS is the author of four books of essays, most recently *The Gutenberg Elegies: The Fate of Reading in an Electronic Age*. He has edited *Tolstoy's Dictaphone: Technology and the Muse*, and a new collection, *Readings*, is forthcoming (Greywolf Press).

ERIC BOLTON taught for some years in Lancashire comprehensive schools before becoming one of Her Majesty's Inspectors of Schools. Between 1983 and 1991, as the Senior Chief Inspector for England and Wales, he was the chief professional adviser on education to the government, and the Head of Her Majesty's Inspectorate. From 1991 to 1996, he was the Professor for Teacher Education at the University of London Institute of Education, and now chairs Book Trust, the Royal Society of Arts' Arts Matters Steering Committee and the Independent Television Commission's Schools Advisory Committee.

A. S. BYATT lectured in English for many years, and was Lecturer and then Senior Lecturer at University College, London, between 1972 and 1983, when she retired from academic life to write full-time. She has been an Associate of Newnham College, Cambridge, since 1977. Her distinguished publications include novels, short stories and literary criticism, and her novel, *Possession,* won the Booker Prize in 1990. She has recently edited *The Oxford Book of Short Stories.*

BRIAN COX retired as John Edward Taylor Professor of English Literature at the University of Manchester in 1993. He co-founded the literary journal *Critical Quarterly* in 1959, and remains on the editorial board as poetry editor. He helped to edit the Black Papers on Education, and in 1988 chaired the National Curriculum English Working Group. He is Chair of the North West Arts Board. He has published numerous articles and books of literary criticism, an autobiography, and several books on education. His *Collected Poems* was published by Carcanet in 1993. In retirement, he edited a two-volume collection of essays, *African Writers,* for Scribner's, selected by the American Library Association as one of the 'Outstanding Reference Sources for 1997'.

VALENTINE CUNNINGHAM is a Professor of English at Oxford and Senior English Tutor at Corpus Christi College. He reviews and broadcasts widely, and is a Permanent Visiting Professor at the University of Konstanz, Germany. His books include *British Writers of the Thirties* (1988) and *In the Reading Gaol: Postmodernity, Texts and History* (1994). He is working on a biography of Dickens for Blackwell.

HENRIETTA DOMBEY is Professor of Literacy in Primary Education at the University of Brighton. While teaching in primary schools for several years in Inner London (and one year in Winchester, Mass.), she developed a keen interest in the learning and teaching of reading. This has been the focus of her subsequent work in teacher education and of her research. She is currently investigating the interactions between teachers and children in successful whole-class literacy lessons. She is a past Chair of the National Association for the Teaching of English.

TERRY FURLONG worked for 20 years in primary and secondary schools in London before becoming an inspector for English. He is an examiner and researcher into examinations and assessment, writes books and teaching materials, and advises on literacy and English. He is a past Chair of the National Association for the Teaching of English, currently chairs the International Federation for the Teaching of English, and is Chair of the Trustees of the English and Media Centre in London.

ROY HATTERSLEY was MP (Labour) for Birmingham, Sparkbrook, from 1964 to 1997, Minister of Defence from 1969 to 1970, Minister of State for Foreign Affairs from 1974 to 1976, Secretary of State for Prices and Consumer Protection from 1976 to 1979, and Deputy Leader of the Labour Party from 1983 to 1992. He was created a Baron (Life Peer) in 1997. He is a very successful journalist with a regular column in the *Guardian*. His many publications include *A Yorkshire Boyhood* (1983) and *Who Goes Home?* (1995), a book about his political career. His next book, *Buster's Diaries* (Buster being Roy's dog) is light-hearted and will be published about the same time as this collection. He is currently writing a biography of William Booth, founder of the Salvation Army.

STEPHEN HEARST has worked for the BBC over four decades, first as television writer/producer, then as head of BBC Television Arts Features. He became Controller, Radio 3, in 1971, and chaired a BBC Think Tank for the four years between 1978 and 1982. He concluded his BBC career as Special Adviser to the Director-General and has since worked as a freelance producer and consultant. He has contributed numerous essays on broadcasting matters to books, periodicals and newspapers.

RICHARD HOGGART is Vice-Chair of Book Trust. His publications run from *Auden* (1951) to *The Way We Live Now* (1995). He founded the Centre for Contemporary Cultural Studies, University of Birmingham, in 1964, and worked as Assistant Director-General of UNESCO in Paris from 1970 to 1975. He was Warden of Goldsmith's College, University of London, from 1976 to 1984.

PADDY LEASE has taught in comprehensive schools in London, Birmingham and Gwent, and lectured in History and Environmental Studies at Swansea College of Higher Education. She has been deputy head at two large comprehensive schools.

DORIS LESSING published her first novel, *The Grass is Singing,* in 1950. Her considerable achievements as a writer stretch through *The Golden Notebook* (1962) to her recent volumes of autobiography. She has been awarded many literary prizes and distinctions. She is President of Book Trust.

COLIN MACCABE was Head of Research, British Film Institutefrom 1989 to 1998 and has been Professor of English, University of Pittsburgh, since 1987. He was previously a Fellow at King's College, Cambridge, from 1976 to 1981, and Professor of English Studies at the University of Strathclyde from 1981 to 1985. His publications include *James Joyce and the Revolution of the Word* (1979) and numerous essays on film, linguistics and literature. He is editor of *Critical Quarterly.*

BETHAN MARSHALL taught in comprehensive schools in Inner London for eight years and worked for a further five as an advisory teacher for English. She is now Lecturer in Education at King's College, London. She writes regularly for the *Guardian* and the *Independent.*

MARGARET MEEK taught in secondary schools over the period of their transformations before becoming Research Fellow at the Universiy of Leeds, and subsequently Lecturer in the Department of Education in the University of Bristol and in the London Institute of Education, where she is now Reader Emeritus. She is the author of *Learning to Read, How Texts Teach What Readers Learn, On Being Literate and Information and Book Learning*, and co-editor of *The Cool Web, Language and Literacy in the Primary School*, and *New Readings*. She is also a member of the executive committee of the National Literacy Trust, and winner of the Eleanor Farjeon Award for services to children's literature.

JANE OGBORN taught for many years in a large comprehensive school in London and eventually became an inspector for English. She has been a Chief Examiner for O Level and GCSE English Literature examinations, and continues to be a coursework moderator for A Level English Literature.

MICHAEL SCHMIDT is Senior Lecturer in English at the University of Manchester, Editorial Director of Carcanet Press and Editor of *PN Review* His most recent book is *Lives of the Poets* (Weidenfeld).

RIVERS SCOTT was a founder member of the *Sunday Telegraph* and its literary editor from 1969 to 1975, when he joined publishers, Hodder and Stoughton as senior editor, non-fiction. He then became literary editor of two more new publications, Sir James Goldsmith's *NOW! Magazine* and the *Mail on Sunday*. In 1981, he and his partner, Gloria Ferris, set up the literary agency Scott Ferris Associates. *No Man is an Island*, a selection of John Donne's prose compiled and introduced by himself, was published by the Folio Society in 1997.

JUDY SIMONS is Dean of the Faculty of Humanities and Social Sciences at De Montfort University, Leicester. She is Chair of the Council for College and University English, the main professional body for Higher Education teachers of English, and is co-author of the 1998 report on *The English Curriculum: Diversity and Standards*. Her most recent publications include *What Katy Read: Feminist Re-Reading of Classic Stories for Girls* (1995), *Mansfield Park and Persuasion: A New Casebook* (1997) and *Writing: A Woman's Business: Women, Writing and the Marketplace* (1998). She is currently working on a history of women's writing for children.

CHRISTOPHER SINCLAIR-STEVENSON began his career as a publisher with Hamish Hamilton in 1961, and became editorial director and then managing editor. When Hamish Hamilton was sold to Penguin he set up his own publishing company, eventually bought by Reed. He now works as a literary agent. His books include *Inglorious Rebellion* (1971) on the Jacobite rebellions, *Blood Royal* (1979) on the Hanoverian dynasty, and *That Sweet Enemy* (1987) on France and the French.

ENID and CHRIS STEPHENSON opened the Hungate Bookshop in Norwich in 1980 and steadily gained a considerable reputation, particularly in the realm of children's books. In 1995, they moved to premises at the Norwich Playhouse which was about to be opened. After barely 18 months the Playhouse closed and the Hungate Bookshop was forced also to close its doors.

JEREMY TREGLOWN is a professor of English at the University of Warwick and chair of the Warwick Writing Programme. Editor of *The Times Literary Supplement* from 1982 to 1990, he has chaired the judges of both the Booker and the Whitbread Prizes. His publications include a biography of Roald Dahl and introductions to all of the novels of Henry Green, about whom he is writing a book.

JOHN WILKS has taught secondary school English in Inner London for 22 years, as well as working as an advisory teacher. He is currently job-sharing a Head of English post in Tower Hamlets and working as the Subject Manager for the PGCE English course at the Urban Learning Foundation, in addition to providing INSET courses for teachers. He is General Secretary of the London Association for the Teaching of English and a National Executive member of the National Association for the Teaching of English.